Praise for *When You Need to Move a Mountain*

"Got a mountain? Want to see it move? Prayer! Our beloved prayer expert, Linda Evans Shepherd, helps us learn to dig deep for the best spiritual excavation in *When You Need to Move a Mountain: Keys to Praying with Power*. We can make a difference through the power of Christ—a difference in the lives of our families and friends, a difference in this world we live in, a God-powered, God-ordained difference even in our own hearts. This book. It's like a manual for glorious faith landscaping!"

Rhonda Rhea, TV personality, humor columnist, and author
of 14 books, including *Messy to Meaningful*, *Fix Her Upper*,
and the award-winning *Turtles in the Road*

"Have you ever had a prayer request so big you were convinced there was no hope for a positive outcome? In *When You Need to Move a Mountain*, Linda Evans Shepherd reveals the secrets of intercessory prayer. She'll teach you how to break strongholds, how to win personal battles, how to protect your family through powerful prayer strategies, and what to do when God says no. This book will transform your life."

Carol Kent, speaker and author, *He Holds My Hand*

"Linda Evans Shepherd is a powerful prayer warrior, so it's no surprise to me that she has written such a power-packed book on prayer! *When You Need to Move a Mountain* is grounded in Scripture and filled with practical suggestions to make your prayer life more effective. If ever there was a time in history when we need prayer warriors to rise up, it is now! May God use this book in your life to compel you to your knees."

Becky Harling, international speaker, leadership coach,
and bestselling author, *How to Listen So People Will Talk*
and *Who Do You Say That I Am?*

"With the wisdom of a Jedi warrior and heart of a mother, Linda Evans Shepherd guides and equips even the novice to understand and persevere in intercessory prayer. Hands-on and practical, *When You Need to Move a Mountain* is part training manual and part motivation to engage in prayers that literally change everything. I wish I'd had this when I was a new believer!"

Julie K. Gillies, author, *From Hot Mess to Blessed*
and *Prayers for a Woman's Soul*

"Everyone faces times in their life when their life circumstances feel like an insurmountable mountain that only a miracle of God can move. Linda has provided a handbook on prayer to help us live in cooperation with God's plans. If you desire to see a God-sized answer or gain guidance from God's Word as you pray, keep this book with your Bible as you hit your knees in prayer."

Pam Farrel, author of 46 books, including bestselling *Discovering Hope in the Psalms: A Creative Bible Study Experience* and *A Couple's Journey with God*

"An expression has been circulating in the Christian community: 'pray small.' Personally, I think God wants us to pray BIG. Jesus healed people of diseases, and he brought people back to life. Our God knows how to give good gifts—and his Son encouraged us to pray prayers that would move mountains. In her newest book on prayer, Linda Shepherd challenges us to pray those mountain-moving prayers, and I highly recommend that you read it and put those big prayers into practice."

Janet Holm McHenry, award-winning speaker and author of 24 books, including the bestselling *PrayerWalk* and her newest, *The Complete Guide to the Prayers of Jesus*

"This book is for everybody who needs to move a mountain. The keys to praying with power will simplify the complicated and fuel your heart with faith to pray so that the mountain is moved. Be ready for an adventure and to see that mountain move."

Monica Schmelter, general manager, WHTN Christian Television Network

"Just when my prayer life seems a little lackluster and routine, I read Linda's book, *When You Need to Move a Mountain*. It's a fresh breath of the Holy Spirit to reenergize your prayer life. She reminds us of many ways to pray and the supernatural power of our almighty miracle-working God to answer prayers. She also shares about types of pray-ers who are called to pray in different ways with different focuses. She provides great tools to energize our prayers. Identifying prayer blockers to overcome, such as sin problems, lack of faith, and forgiveness issues allows readers to address those issues and become effective prayer warriors."

Karen Whiting, author, international speaker, former TV host, and Bible study teacher

Praying
THROUGH
Every Emotion

Books by Linda Evans Shepherd

Praying God's Promises

Empowered for Purpose: Winning Your Daily Spiritual Battles

Called to Pray: Astounding Stories of Answered Prayer

How to Pray in Times of Stress

When You Don't Know What to Pray:
How to Talk to God about Anything

How to Pray When You Need a Miracle

Experiencing God's Presence: Learning to Listen While You Pray

When You Need to Move a Mountain: Keys to Praying with Power

Praying through Hard Times: Finding Strength in God's Presence

Novels

The Potluck Club

The Potluck Club—Trouble's Brewing

The Potluck Club—Takes the Cake

The Secret's in the Sauce

A Taste of Fame

Bake Until Golden

Praying
THROUGH
Every Emotion

Experiencing God's Peace
No Matter What

Linda Evans Shepherd

a division of Baker Publishing Group
Grand Rapids, Michigan

© 2021 by Linda Evans Shepherd

Published by Revell
a division of Baker Publishing Group
PO Box 6287, Grand Rapids, MI 49516-6287
www.revellbooks.com

Printed in the United States of America

Library of Congress Cataloging-in-Publication Data
Names: Shepherd, Linda E., 1957– author.
Title: Praying through every emotion : experiencing God's peace no matter what / Linda
    Evans Shepherd.
Description: Grand Rapids, Michigan : Revell, a division of Baker Publishing Group, 2021.
Identifiers: LCCN 2020019536 | ISBN 9780800738402
Subjects: LCSH: Prayers. | Emotions—Religious aspects—Christianity—Miscellanea. |
    Bible—Quotations.
Classification: LCC BV260 .S455 2020 | DDC 248.3/2—dc23
LC record available at https://lccn.loc.gov/2020019536

Scripture quotations labeled ESV are from The Holy Bible, English Standard Version® (ESV®), copyright © 2001 by Crossway, a publishing ministry of Good News Publishers. Used by permission. All rights reserved. ESV Text Edition: 2016

Scripture quotations labeled GNT are from the Good News Translation in Today's English Version-Second Edition. Copyright © 1992 by American Bible Society. Used by permission.

Scripture quotations labeled GW are from GOD'S WORD, a copyrighted work of God's Word to the Nations. Quotations are used by permission. Copyright © 1995 by God's Word to the Nations. All rights reserved.

Scripture quotations labeled KJV are from the King James Version of the Bible.

Scripture quotations labeled MSG are from THE MESSAGE, copyright © 1993, 1994, 1995, 1996, 2000, 2001, 2002 by Eugene H. Peterson. Used by permission of NavPress. All rights reserved. Represented by Tyndale House Publishers, Inc.

Scripture quotations labeled NET are from the NET Bible®, copyright © 1996–2016 by Biblical Studies Press, L.L.C. http://netbible.com. Used by permission. All rights reserved.

Scripture quotations labeled NIV are from the Holy Bible, New International Version®. NIV®. Copyright © 1973, 1978, 1984, 2011 by Biblica, Inc.™ Used by permission of Zondervan. All rights reserved worldwide. www.zondervan.com. The "NIV" and "New International Version" are trademarks registered in the United States Patent and Trademark Office by Biblica, Inc.™

Scripture quotations labeled NKJV are from the New King James Version®. Copyright © 1982 by Thomas Nelson. Used by permission. All rights reserved.

Scripture quotations labeled NLT are from the Holy Bible, New Living Translation, copyright © 1996, 2004, 2007, 2013, 2015 by Tyndale House Foundation. Used by permission of Tyndale House Publishers, Inc., Carol Stream, Illinois 60188. All rights reserved.

Scripture quotations labeled NLV are taken from the New Life Version, copyright © 1969 and 2003. Used by permission of Barbour Publishing, Inc., Uhrichsville, Ohio 44683. All rights reserved.

Scripture quotations labeled PHILLIPS are from the New Testament in Modern English by J. B. Phillips copyright © 1960, 1972 J. B. Phillips. Administered by The Archbishops' Council of the Church of England. Used by Permission.

Scripture quotations labeled TPT are from the Passion Translation®. Copyright © 2017 by BroadStreet Publishing® Group, LLC. Used by permission. All rights reserved.

Scripture quotations labeled VOICE are from The Voice™. Copyright © 2008 by Ecclesia Bible Society. Used by permission. All rights reserved.

Published in association with Books & Such Literary Management. www.booksandsuch.com.

For my readers

But the Holy Spirit produces this kind of fruit in our lives: love, joy, peace, patience, kindness, goodness, faithfulness, gentleness, and self-control. There is no law against these things!

Galatians 5:22–23 NLT

Contents

Introduction

The LORD is near to everyone who prays to him,
  to every faithful person who prays to him.
He fills the needs of those who fear him.
  He hears their cries for help and saves them.
The LORD protects everyone who loves him.

Psalm 145:18–20 GW

It had been a difficult day.

Well, a difficult week.

Let's make that a hard month.

To be truthful, it had been a crazy, unrelenting year—a year in which I had taken a ride on the roller coaster of angst and ridden a whirlwind of anxiety. I had experienced stress, disappointments, betrayals, worries, grief, isolation, and family trauma. It was a year that had left me sinking into the muck of this world.

But this particular day had been extra difficult. It was as if I had experienced an emotional hurricane triggered by the swell of exciting news, followed by news that shocked and angered me, followed by news that left me stressed and bewildered.

By the end of the day, I felt like a storm had raged through my heart, leaving behind a high-water mark of frustration. Where was my peace? Where was my joy? But beyond that, where was my quiet trust in God?

Can you relate?

If so, you've come to the right place, because I am about to share the prayer that brought me back to peace:

Dear Lord,

My emotions are twisted in so many knots that I can't even process all that's happened today. So even though this doesn't seem to be a fair exchange, I'm asking You to trade my emotional turmoil for Your peace that passes understanding.

Thank You!

In the name of Jesus, amen.

I took a deep breath and began to let go, giving it all to God. I felt the cares of the world drain off my mind and my soul. I knew God was with me, and His Spirit began to flow peace into my spirit. And I knew everything would be all right, maybe not according to my timeline but definitely according to His.

I was back to peace.

Finding peace is the aim when praying through emotions. It's not about learning how to control your circumstances; it's about learning how to release your circumstances to the One who loves you, the One you can trust.

So join me in this prayer adventure as I share with you some of my favorite prayers for praying through emotions so that you can push into the peace that passes understanding.

May His peace be with you.

Love,
Linda Evans Shepherd

P.S. There are many ways you can use this book. You can read it straight through as a devotional, or you can consult the contents page to find prayers you need for your life right now.

As you pray, you'll discover that the prayers are a reflection or a paraphrase of the accompanying Scripture passages. This was by design, because God loves it when we pray His Word to Him. His Word is alive and filled with power; it strengthens our souls and brings peace to our emotions. Praying God's Word also gives us the confidence that we are not only praying in His will but also agreeing with and activating His promises to us.

Be sure to linger over the Scripture passages that go with each prayer, because God's Word is the source of transforming power. When you find a Scripture passage that speaks to you, read it again. Then use that passage to craft a prayer of your own back to the Lord. This is a way not only to continue praying but also to experience and rest in God's presence.

When you find a prayer that has deep meaning to you, pray the prayer often. Consider meditating on and even memorizing the Scripture passages that accompany it so that you can recall them whenever you need them.

And don't be afraid to read prayers that concern emotions you don't relate to right now, because the moment may come when you will need the peace those prayers will provide. Also, seek out and enjoy the inspirational prayers, like the prayers concerning victory, worship, and faith, for those prayers were created for you to grow in your fellowship with the God who loves you.

Be sure to keep an extra copy of *Praying through Every Emotion* on hand so you always have one to give to a friend or loved one.

God bless you, and let your prayer adventure begin.

Addicted

Dear Lord,
  You did not create me to be a slave to addiction. So when addiction's tentacles pull me beneath the waves, give me Your name as a lifeline so I can break free from my tug-of-war with death.

Even now, Your gaze is steady on my face as I focus on You. We walk arm in arm as You lead me from the lure of temptation and deliver me from evil.

Others have escaped these same temptations because of Your faithfulness. You are also faithful to me! You show me how to endure when temptations call me to go under.

I will no longer be drunk with wine, because You, O Lord, are filling my cup with Your very presence. I am no longer empty, craving what would destroy me, for I am now filled with Your power. Fill me even more with Your power and help me to be sober and on alert to the enemy's attacks.

Through Your power, I say no to the call of addiction and yes to You. Lord, Your grace calls me to experience Your glory in Christ. Yes, I have suffered, but You are continually restoring me to Yourself, and now I am strong, firm, and steadfast, all because of You. I turn to You as I step away from the things that formerly held me captive and declare my freedom through the power of the blood of Jesus.

In the name of Jesus, amen.

It is for freedom that Christ has set us free. Stand firm, then, and do not let yourselves be burdened again by a yoke of slavery.

Galatians 5:1 NIV

And lead us not into temptation,
    but deliver us from the evil one.
Matthew 6:13 NIV

God is faithful. He will not allow the temptation to be more than you can stand. When you are tempted, he will show you a way out so that you can endure.

1 Corinthians 10:13 NLT

Don't be drunk with wine, because that will ruin your life. Instead, be filled with the Holy Spirit.

Ephesians 5:18 NLT

Be alert and of sober mind. Your enemy the devil prowls around like a roaring lion looking for someone to devour. Resist him, standing firm in the faith, because you know that the family of believers throughout the world is undergoing the same kind of sufferings. And the God of all grace, who called you to his eternal glory in Christ, after you have suffered a little while, will himself restore you and make you strong, firm and steadfast.

1 Peter 5:8–10 NIV

Angry

Dear Lord,

I'm angry, outraged, and I want to use my words to punch someone hard.

If I'm the one in the right and my opponent is in the wrong, how can I justify stupidity or unjust opposition?

I hear Your silence, so I humble myself before You. As I do, I feel Your quiet. You, the God of truth and justice, will help me to stand strong without sinning.

Help me not to let my anger tempt me to engage in foolish and stupid arguments that lead to quarrels. Give me the strength to be kind, to be patient, and even to suffer wrongs when I stand up for You.

Show me how to be gentle when I correct those who misunderstand or oppose the truth so that my example attracts my opponents to You.

Because You love me, teach me how to lay down my pride so that I can be humble, gentle, and patient. Remind me to invite Your presence into every situation.

I push my pride aside and extend an invitation to You and Your amazing love to join me in this conflict now. Help me to be kind and to choose my words carefully, never in haste. Show me how to be slow to become angry so that I can achieve Your righteous purpose.

Give me the ability to love with Your love.

In the name of Jesus, amen.

Be ye angry, and sin not: let not the sun go down upon your wrath.

Ephesians 4:26 KJV

Don't have anything to do with foolish and stupid arguments. You know they cause quarrels. A servant of the Lord must not quarrel. Instead, he must be kind to everyone. He must be a good teacher. He must be willing to suffer wrong. He must be gentle in correcting those who oppose the Good News. Maybe God will allow them to change the way they think and act and lead them to know the truth.

2 Timothy 2:23–25 GW

Be humble. Be gentle. Be patient. Tolerate one another in an atmosphere thick with love.

Ephesians 4:2 VOICE

Everyone must be quick to listen, but slow to speak and slow to become angry. Human anger does not achieve God's righteous purpose.

James 1:19–20 GNT

Annoyed

Dear Lord,

Help! I'm in the middle of a love deficit.

I've tried to stretch my patience, but annoyance pulls me tight like a rubber band and I snap.

I ask that You remind me of Your love for me. In fact, I open my heart to receive more of Your love, because when I recognize Your love for me, Your love fills my heart, creating a love reserve that covers all irritating people.

When I have Your love flowing to me, then through me, I have patience. I am kind. I'm never jealous, haughty, arrogant, or rude. I am able to think of others without annoyance. I stop keeping my list of their wrongs. I am even able to encourage and care for those I tried to dismiss, ignore, or avoid.

But the best part? I don't run out of patience and never give up on others because Your love supply never ends.

Your love makes me beautiful with gentleness. Your love clothes me with a good attitude and helps me to bear with those You have put in my life, even to the point of forgiving them.

Keep my heart filled with Your love so I can stretch and never snap.

In the name of Jesus, amen.

Your beauty should be a gentle and quiet spirit. In God's sight this is of great worth and no amount of money can buy it.

1 Peter 3:4 NLV

Love is patient. Love is kind. Love isn't jealous. It doesn't sing its own praises. It isn't arrogant. It isn't rude. It doesn't think about itself. It isn't irritable. It doesn't keep track of wrongs. It isn't happy when injustice is done, but it is happy with the truth. Love never stops being patient, never stops believing, never stops hoping, never gives up. Love never comes to an end.

1 Corinthians 13:4–8 GW

Above all, love each other warmly, because love covers many sins.

1 Peter 4:8 GW

Therefore, as God's chosen people, holy and dearly loved, clothe yourselves with compassion, kindness, humility, gentleness and patience. Bear with each other and forgive one another if any of you has a grievance against someone. Forgive as the Lord forgave you.

Colossians 3:12–13 NIV

Anxious

Dear Lord,

The trouble in this world has made me anxious. But You want me to turn my anxieties over to You. You remind me not to fear or be dismayed because You are my God. You promise to strengthen and help me as You hold my hand.

Okay, I'll take Your anxiety challenge and give You all my anxieties. I turn over my life, my food, my clothes, my body, my fears, and my worries to You.

After all, the birds never worry or stress out about their lives, and You take wonderful care of them. And you've said that I'm more important to You than the birds.

My anxiety has been unproductive, causing my head to spin as I search for impossible solutions instead of trusting You.

But the solutions are not up to me. The solutions to my problems belong to You. You can figure everything out so much better than I can even imagine. All I have to say is "Thank You!"

I declare that You are in charge of my problems. I trust You to show me what to do in every situation as You put me on the right path. I give You my hand and take a deep breath as I realize You've got this. You've got all of it. I will trust You every day—remembering that You are the Lord over all and especially over me.

In the name of Jesus, amen.

Turn all your anxiety over to God because he cares for you.

1 Peter 5:7 GW

So do not fear, for I am with you;
  do not be dismayed, for I am your God.
I will strengthen you and help you;
  I will uphold you with my righteous right hand.

Isaiah 41:10 NIV

Therefore I tell you, do not be anxious about your life, what you will eat or what you will drink, nor about your body, what you will put on. Is not life more than food, and the body more than clothing? Look at the birds of the air: they neither sow nor reap nor gather into barns, and yet your heavenly Father feeds them. Are you not of more value than they?

Matthew 6:25–26 ESV

Trust in the LORD with all your heart;
  do not depend on your own understanding.
Seek his will in all you do,
  and he will show you which path to take.

Proverbs 3:5–6 NLT

Betrayed

Dear Lord,

Wow! I did not see that coming. And I have to ask, is my so-called friend's "blade" still in my back?

This is so painful and unfair, Lord. In fact, I think this would be a good time for me to take revenge. But that's not how You want me to react.

I do like the fact that You want to take care of this betrayal Yourself, because as You say, You alone have the right to revenge. You even promise to "pay betrayal back," which may be a bit frightening, especially to those who deceived me.

But, Jesus, may I never forget that You forgave Your betrayers, even while You suffered on the cross. Is that why You want me to forgive, to bless and not to curse?

Lord, I'll follow Your example. Please forgive them, bless them, and do not curse them. But this I ask: please do not let these people or their actions put me to shame.

You've made a few promises to me when it comes to betrayal. You promise to bless me when people mock me and persecute me and tell evil lies about me because I follow You. You tell me to rejoice because You will give me a great reward.

Even now, You reward me by preparing a feast for me in the presence of my enemies. You honor me by anointing me with Your Holy Spirit. And thank You that despite everything, my cup overflows with blessings.

In the name of Jesus, amen.

Don't take revenge, dear friends. Instead, let God's anger take
care of it. After all, Scripture says, "I alone have the right to take
revenge. I will pay back, says the Lord."

Romans 12:19 GW

Bless those who persecute you. Bless them, and don't curse them.

Romans 12:14 GW

I trust you, O my God.
Do not let me be put to shame.
Do not let my enemies triumph over me.

Psalm 25:2 GW

God blesses you when people mock you and persecute you and
lie about you and say all sorts of evil things against you because
you are my followers. Be happy about it! Be very glad! For a great
reward awaits you in heaven.

Matthew 5:11–12 NLT

You prepare a feast for me
in the presence of my enemies.
You honor me by anointing my head with oil.
My cup overflows with blessings.

Psalm 23:5 NLT

Bitter

Dear Lord,

I'm brooding, rehashing, and building my case against the one who wronged me. I keep thinking about what I should have said, wishing I'd slung zingers in the moment instead of only thinking of them now.

My outrage makes it hard to hear You. It's like the more I try to justify my bitterness, the less I feel your presence. It's as though my bitter thoughts are poisoning my soul with arsenic.

That's not what I want. I don't want to turn against Your grace, especially because I know that Your Word says You won't forgive me if I won't forgive others. That sounds harsh until I feel the weight of my own sin. It's just as nasty as the sin against me. When I indulge in bitterness, the blame I point at others points right back to me.

So out of my love for You, Lord, I give You this situation and ask for You to turn it around. And while I'm at it, I give You all my dirty laundry—my bitterness, rage, anger, fighting, slander, and malice. In exchange, give me Your power to be kind, compassionate, and forgiving, just as You've forgiven me.

Bitterness has no place in my life because Your love (in me) will cover every wrong. Your power (in me) will give me the strength to forgive not only others but even myself. Thank You, Lord.

In the name of Jesus, amen.

Guard against turning back from the grace of God. Let no one become like a bitter plant that grows up and causes many troubles with its poison.

Hebrews 12:15 GNT

If you forgive the failures of others, your heavenly Father will also forgive you. But if you don't forgive others, your Father will not forgive your failures.

Matthew 6:14–15 GW

Don't say, "I will get even for this wrong."
Wait for the LORD to handle the matter.
Proverbs 20:22 NLT

Get rid of all bitterness, rage and anger, brawling and slander, along with every form of malice. Be kind and compassionate to one another, forgiving each other, just as in Christ God forgave you.

Ephesians 4:31–32 NIV

Hate starts quarrels,
but love covers every wrong.
Proverbs 10:12 GW

Blessed

Dear Lord,

You promise that if I trust and put my confidence in You, I will be blessed. But how blessed do I have to be before I feel blessed?

Your way of blessing me is not what I expected.

You say that when I am poor, I am blessed because I realize I need You, and You promise me the kingdom of heaven. You say that when I am humble, my inheritance is the whole earth. You say that when I am hungry and thirsty for justice, I will be satisfied. You promise to bless me with mercy when I am merciful to others.

You bless me when my need causes me to seek You more. When I seek You more, I will find You and You will continue to bless me.

Finding You is the biggest blessing I can have.

Because I know You, You prevent me from falling into worldly traps as I continue to seek You through Your Word.

I am blessed because when I reflect on Your teachings I become like a tree nourished in rich soil and refreshed by bubbling streams. My leaves will never wither, and I will produce fruit in season.

When I am blessed in this way, You promise me success in everything I do because I am doing it with and for You. So, Lord, please bless me! I want to be blessed, and I want to be a blessing to You.

In the name of Jesus, amen.

But blessed is the one who trusts in the LORD,
    whose confidence is in him.

Jeremiah 17:7 NIV

God blesses those who are poor and realize their need
      for him,
    for the Kingdom of Heaven is theirs.
God blesses those who mourn,
    for they will be comforted.
God blesses those who are humble,
    for they will inherit the whole earth.
God blesses those who hunger and thirst for justice,
    for they will be satisfied.
God blesses those who are merciful,
    for they will be shown mercy.

Matthew 5:3–7 NLT

Blessed is the person who does not follow the advice
      of wicked people,
    take the path of sinners, or join the company of
      mockers.
Rather, he delights in the teachings of the LORD
    and reflects on his teachings day and night.
He is like a tree planted beside streams—
    a tree that produces fruit in season and whose leaves
      do not wither.
He succeeds in everything he does.

Psalm 1:1–3 GW

Bold

Dear Lord,

Why does my heart pound? Why do my knees knock? Have I forgotten that I belong to You? I do not need to approach life as though I'm a sneaky thief, afraid of being caught. I do not need to flee whenever someone notices me or knows what I stand for, especially when I am standing in You and Your righteousness.

Fear will not stop me. I will face my life and my call with the boldness of a lion, for You have commanded me to be strong of heart. There is no need for me to be afraid or to lose faith, for You are with me wherever I go.

Whether I'm young or grayed and wrinkled, I will go wherever You command me. I will not be afraid of the people I must face, for You are with me and You will rescue me.

Because I belong to You, Your very Spirit is in me, and Your Spirit is not timid, so neither am I! Your Spirit fills me with power, love, and self-control.

I can be a person of hope who is bold in You. Give me Your power to be bolder still so that I can do whatever I need to do, whatever You call me to do. I declare that fear will not hold me back from receiving and following Your call on my life.

In the name of Jesus, amen.

A wicked person flees when no one is chasing him,
but righteous people are as bold as lions.

Proverbs 28:1 GW

Have I not told you? Be strong and have strength of heart! Do not be afraid or lose faith. For the Lord your God is with you anywhere you go.

Joshua 1:9 NLV

But the LORD said to me, "Do not say, 'I am too young.' You must go to everyone I send you to and say whatever I command you. Do not be afraid of them, for I am with you and will rescue you," declares the LORD.

Jeremiah 1:7–8 NIV

For the Spirit that God has given us does not make us timid; instead, his Spirit fills us with power, love, and self-control.

2 Timothy 1:7 GNT

Therefore, since we have such a hope, we are very bold.

2 Corinthians 3:12 NIV

Broken

Dear Lord,

This world is filled with difficulties, and sometimes my battle scars and life wounds make me feel as though I can't continue the fight. In those times, my heart feels broken, and my mind wants to surrender to the pain.

But even in these darkest of moments, when I cry out to You, You hear me and rescue me. Whenever I think of Your greatness, I remember that You are near. As I look back on battles of the past, I can see You've saved me time and again. Though I've had more than a few troubles, You've rescued me from them all.

When the tide comes in like a flood and I fear I will drown, when the water is over my head, You are with me and You pull me to safety. When I have to cross swift rivers, You keep me afloat.

I am never burned by the fires set by the enemy, and his flames never destroy me. My fire insurance is that I trust You. I know You will repay and restore what the enemy has devoured in my life.

You are close to me when my heart is broken, and You save me when my spirit is crushed.

I can come to You whenever I'm exhausted from carrying heavy burdens, and You will give me rest. I need Your rest now. Once again, restore my soul and make me whole.

In the name of Jesus, amen.

Righteous people cry out.
   The LORD hears and rescues them from all their
      troubles.
The LORD is near to those whose hearts are humble.
   He saves those whose spirits are crushed.
The righteous person has many troubles,
   but the LORD rescues him from all of them.

Psalm 34:17–19 GW

When you go through deep water,
   I will be with you.
When you go through rivers of difficulty,
   you will not drown.
When you walk through the fire of oppression,
   you will not be burned up;
   the flames will not consume you.

Isaiah 43:2 NLT

I will repay you for the years the locusts have eaten.

Joel 2:25 NIV

The LORD is close to the brokenhearted
   and saves those who are crushed in spirit.

Psalm 34:18 NIV

Come to me, all you who are weary and burdened, and I will
give you rest.

Matthew 11:28 NIV

Burdened

Dear Lord,

When I can't feel Your presence, when Your Spirit feels far way, I feel exhausted. I'm worn-out, unable to do all You've called me to do.

That's when You whisper to me, "Come! Come and spend time with Me. Open My Word. Think of My greatness and My care for You."

Spending time with You, acknowledging You are with me, is the only way I can find rest from the drudge. When I am walking with You, I know You are walking with me. That's when I see that You are doing the heavy lifting. Not me!

You never burden me. You undergird me with Your strong hands and teach me how to live freely, unbound by the chains of the world. You teach me how to travel lightly down the path You have for my life.

When I try to carry my burdens by myself, I end up with a backache that won't quit. That's why I give my burdens to You. You carry them and keep me from stumbling under their weight.

I place my burdens in Your care and thank You for carrying them. You have saved me, and You also show me how to help others with their burdens. I will do all You show me to do because I belong to You and because doing what You ask always turns out to be a blessing.

In the name of Jesus, amen.

Are you tired? Worn out? Burned out on religion? Come to me. Get away with me and you'll recover your life. I'll show you how to take a real rest. Walk with me and work with me—watch how I do it. Learn the unforced rhythms of grace. I won't lay anything heavy or ill-fitting on you. Keep company with me and you'll learn to live freely and lightly.

Matthew 11:28–30 MSG

Give your burdens to the LORD,
    and he will take care of you.
    He will not permit the godly to slip and fall.

Psalm 55:22 NLT

Praise the Lord,
    who carries our burdens day after day;
    he is the God who saves us.

Psalm 68:19 GNT

Help carry each other's burdens. In this way you will follow Christ's teachings.

Galatians 6:2 GW

Compassionate

Dear Lord,

You love me and call me to funnel Your love into everything I do.

Help me to live the kind of life You've called me to live with Your gifts of humility, gentleness, and patience so that I can lovingly accept others the way You accept me.

Help me to be kind and also forgiving, just as Christ forgave me. Help me to love my brothers and sisters with tenderheartedness and to be courteous to all.

I ask You to help me see the needs around me so I can share compassion with those I love and those even beyond my own circle. Show me when and how to reach out to the hungry and the hurting. Pure religion is not practiced in church but whenever I see and attend to widows, orphans, and others in need.

Help me to remain uncorrupted by the world. Keep me from becoming jaded. Show me how to use compassion as a secret weapon to help others defeat the devourer. May those with whom I share compassion grow in love so that they can turn and share Your compassion with others. In this way, allow Your gift of compassion to become an endless gift throughout the generations.

I want to live my life in and through Your love.

In the name of Jesus, amen.

Do everything with love.

1 Corinthians 16:14 GW

Live the kind of life which proves that God has called you. Be humble and gentle in every way. Be patient with each other and lovingly accept each other.

Ephesians 4:1–2 GW

Be kind and compassionate to one another, forgiving each other, just as in Christ God forgave you.

Ephesians 4:32 NIV

Finally, all of you be of one mind, having compassion for one another; love as brothers, be tenderhearted, be courteous.

1 Peter 3:8 NKJV

Pure and genuine religion in the sight of God the Father means caring for orphans and widows in their distress and refusing to let the world corrupt you.

James 1:27 NLT

Confident

*D*ear Lord,

When I imagine myself alone, without You, I lose hope. What power do I have to win life's battles without You? But why worry about such a thing when You are always with me?

I am traveling through this life with You, my powerful God who is living on the inside of me. What a wonder and a miracle that is!

You are the God of peace who protects me from the schemes of the devil. You crush him beneath my feet because the grace of my Lord Jesus is over me. And for this reason alone, I have the strength to face anything that comes my way through the power of Christ.

I am confident that You have already begun a good work in me. I know You will carry this good work to completion until the day I meet Jesus face-to-face.

This is why I have the confidence to say, "Lord, You are my helper. I have no need to fear. I am under Your power and authority. My soul cannot be touched by anything anyone tries to do to me because I am in You and I am Yours."

Even though I cannot yet see You face-to-face, I know You are with me. Because I know You and because Your grace has covered my sin, I will enjoy Your peace that quiets my soul. My confidence is in You forever.

In the name of Jesus, amen.

The God of peace will soon crush Satan under your feet. The grace of our Lord Jesus be with you.

Romans 16:20 NIV

I have the strength to face all conditions by the power that Christ gives me.

Philippians 4:13 GNT

Being confident of this, that he who began a good work in you will carry it on to completion until the day of Christ Jesus.

Philippians 1:6 NIV

So we can confidently say,

> "The Lord is my helper;
>   I will not fear;
> what can man do to me?"

Hebrews 13:6 ESV

To have faith is to be sure of the things we hope for, to be certain of the things we cannot see.

Hebrews 11:1 GNT

> The fruit of that righteousness will be peace;
>   its effect will be quietness and confidence forever.

Isaiah 32:17 NIV

Confused

*D*ear Lord,

Your Word says that there's more than one spirit in the world. I know the Spirit of truth comes from You. But there's another spirit who comes to confuse me, who schemes to steal, kill, and destroy my soul. Help me to avoid that evil imitator so I can stay under Your guidance, my true and loving God.

Your Spirit is easy to discern because the Holy Spirit acknowledges Christ as Lord. He guards my heart and soul from the enemy. O Lord, You give me wisdom instead of confusion. You give me peace instead of fear.

Your Holy Spirit comes to guide me in all Your truth. My spirit hears from Your Spirit and tells me the insights I need to know to take the right paths.

Lord, I want more of Your presence. I know that when I ask, I will receive. You are found when I search for You. When I knock at Your door, You open it wide.

As I become more intimate with Your Spirit of truth, I will flourish in Your love. I will have better understanding and will be able to make better decisions because I will recognize the difference between the evil one and Your Holy Spirit. I will be able to follow You and remain pure and blameless for Christ.

Please give me more of Your Holy Spirit so that I can always discern Your truth.

In the name of Jesus, amen.

Dear friends, do not believe every spirit, but test the spirits to see whether they are from God, because many false prophets have gone out into the world.

1 John 4:1 NIV

For God is not a God of confusion but of peace.

1 Corinthians 14:33 ESV

But when he, the Spirit of truth, comes, he will guide you into all the truth. He will not speak on his own; he will speak only what he hears, and he will tell you what is yet to come.

John 16:13 NIV

Ask, and you will receive. Search, and you will find. Knock, and the door will be opened for you.

Matthew 7:7 GW

And this is my prayer: that your love may abound more and more in knowledge and depth of insight, so that you may be able to discern what is best and may be pure and blameless for the day of Christ.

Philippians 1:9–10 NIV

Content

Dear Lord,

You taught us to watch out, to keep away from wanting things we should not have. This is because our lives are not about the stuff we collect but about distributing Your love.

My life has far more importance than the knickknacks I'll leave behind when I die. Your kingdom has no need for my trash. I am called to expand Your kingdom in ways that have Your stamp of approval, like loving my neighbors, caring for those in need, telling the good news, and loving You with all my heart.

You promise that if I work for You, You will provide everything I need. The apostle Paul taught us to be content in every situation, whether having nothing or everything, whether fed or hungry, whether having plenty or little.

My wealth does not come from gathering more things but from the godly contentment I experience when I am satisfied with what You provide.

There is a beauty in recognizing Your provision instead of focusing on what I want. When I focus on Your blessings, I am satisfied, but when I focus on what I want, I am always in need.

It's impossible to love money and be content, for my wealth is not in a bank account but in You. I am wealthy because You promise that You will never abandon or leave me.

When I have You, I am rich indeed.

In the name of Jesus, amen.

Then Jesus said to them all, "Watch yourselves! Keep from wanting all kinds of things you should not have. A man's life is not made up of things, even if he has many riches."

Luke 12:15 NLV

But first, be concerned about his kingdom and what has his approval. Then all these things will be provided for you.

Matthew 6:33 GW

I know how to live on almost nothing or with everything. I have learned the secret of living in every situation, whether it is with a full stomach or empty, with plenty or little.

Philippians 4:12 NLT

Yet true godliness with contentment is itself great wealth. After all, we brought nothing with us when we came into the world, and we can't take anything with us when we leave it. So if we have enough food and clothing, let us be content.

1 Timothy 6:6–8 NLT

Don't love money. Be happy with what you have because God has said, "I will never abandon you or leave you."

Hebrews 13:5 GW

Cynical

Dear Lord,

Sometimes I see the dark underbelly of situations, people, attitudes, and behaviors, and when I do, I want to explain what I see—so that others will see things my way too. I convince myself that my insights paired with my grumbled whispers and complaints will improve everything.

I mutter, "Why don't they see it my way, do it my way, or ask me my opinion?"

When I act like this, I'm pointing to my own pride and hypocrisy as well as my own bitter heart. This unwise behavior opens a door for You to judge me.

I am so sorry, and I turn away from this behavior. Create a loving heart in me, and forgive me so that I do not judge others or forget to speak in love. Help me to show mercy and grace so that I can receive Your mercy and grace. Otherwise I am blinded by my own pride.

I call for mercy and grace over all whom I have grumbled against. I ask that You remove my bitter words against them and remove Your bitter judgments against me. Give me eyes to see Your love and grace in every situation and individual You have called me to influence. Help me to love others as You have loved me.

I invite You to turn every situation that has annoyed me into a situation that honors You. I pledge to encourage others instead of condemning them. I pledge to speak words of love.

In the name of Jesus, amen.

Speak only what is good so that you can give help wherever it is needed. That way, what you say will help those who hear you.

Ephesians 4:29 GW

Brothers and sisters, stop complaining about each other, or you will be condemned. Realize that the judge is standing at the door.

James 5:9 GW

Judge not, that you be not judged. For with the judgment you pronounce you will be judged, and with the measure you use it will be measured to you. Why do you see the speck that is in your brother's eye, but do not notice the log that is in your own eye? Or how can you say to your brother, "Let me take the speck out of your eye," when there is the log in your own eye? You hypocrite, first take the log out of your own eye, and then you will see clearly to take the speck out of your brother's eye.

Matthew 7:1–5 ESV

Depressed

*D*ear Lord,
    I know that everyone gets tired and depressed at some point in their lives, but I don't want to live in the state of depression. So, I choose You. I choose to trust You, not my feelings.

You promise that if I hope in You, You will renew my strength. Lord, by faith, I am hoping in You now. Help me to soar on wings like eagles, run and not grow weary, and walk and not faint.

Lord, You are eternal, and Your arms are not only holding me close but also helping me to soar above my hurting emotions.

Your Word says three things: first, You go before me; second, You are with me; and third, You are faithful to me. You will never leave me to face life alone. That's why I don't need to be afraid, depressed, or troubled.

You, O Lord, are the wings beneath me and a shield around me, protecting me from the evil one. Because I ask You in the name of Jesus, You cancel the enemy's plans of depression over me and lift my spirit as I look into Your loving, peaceful eyes.

I seek You now. I give You my burdens now. Thank You for carrying them so that I can rest in You.

I choose to stop focusing on my wounded emotions and choose to focus on Your love for me. I will bask in Your love as I open my spirit to more of You.

In the name of Jesus, amen.

Even youths grow tired and weary,
and young men stumble and fall;
but those who hope in the Lord
will renew their strength.
They will soar on wings like eagles;
they will run and not grow weary,
they will walk and not be faint.

Isaiah 40:30–31 NIV

The God Who lives forever is your safe place. His arms are always under you.

Deuteronomy 33:27 NLV

The Lord is the One Who goes before you. He will be with you. He will be faithful to you and will not leave you alone. Do not be afraid or troubled.

Deuteronomy 31:8 NLV

But you, O Lord, are a shield about me,
my glory, and the lifter of my head.

Psalm 3:3 ESV

Then Jesus said, "Come to me, all of you who are weary and carry heavy burdens, and I will give you rest."

Matthew 11:28 NLT

Devoted

Dear Lord,

Thank You, Jesus, for dying in my place for my sins. Thank You for calling me to belong to You. What an honor and a privilege to have my sins removed so that I can not only walk with You but also know You.

Lord, I respond to Your marvelous mercies by totally surrendering myself to You as a sacred, living sacrifice. I devote myself to You and pledge to live in holiness, turning from darkness to light and surrendering my old way of life to You. Because I devote myself to You as my true worship, I will experience all that delights Your heart.

I will worship You alone. I will not worship both You and the god of money. Worshiping money would only lead me to resent You and to become a slave to my desires or ambitions.

I declare that You are the one I serve. And to prove it, I will honor You with my wealth and the first part of all my income. I will fear only You, Lord, and I will be faithful to keeping my focus on You, the one I worship. I will meditate on the great things You have done for me.

You have given me salvation, love, and even Your very presence. You are my God, and I am devoted to You with all my heart.

In the name of Jesus, amen.

You are among those who have been called to belong to Jesus Christ.

Romans 1:6 GW

Beloved friends, what should be our proper response to God's marvelous mercies? I encourage you to surrender yourselves to God to be his sacred, living sacrifices. And live in holiness, experiencing all that delights his heart. For this becomes your genuine expression of worship.

Romans 12:1 TPT

How could you worship two gods at the same time? You will have to hate one and love the other, or be devoted to one and despise the other. You can't worship the true God while enslaved to the god of money!

Matthew 6:24 TPT

Honor the LORD with your wealth
and with the first and best part of all your income.

Proverbs 3:9 GW

Only fear the Lord and be faithful to worship Him with all your heart. Think of the great things He has done for you.

1 Samuel 12:24 NLV

Disappointed

Dear Lord,

If You have all these great plans for me, plans for peace that include a future and a hope, why do I have so much disappointment?

I love You, Lord, but sometimes I fail to understand Your Word. Romans 8:28 declares that You will take *all* that happens to me and work it for my good. But aren't You supposed to be a loving God? Why would You want to torment me with so many disappointments?

Still, I can't help but wonder . . . what if it takes the roadblocks of disappointment to prompt me to seek Your help or to consider Your direction? What if You are loving and powerful enough to turn the very details of my disappointments into miracles?

I believe in You, so I surrender to You. I will be strong and courageous as I wait on You, the one true God.

The dark rulers of this world do not love me; they intend to use my disappointments for evil and distraction. But You intend to use my disappointments for purpose and good.

So I will trust in You. The vision You have for me will happen at the appointed time. The aim is already set. Your goal is to hit the bull's-eye. Even if I must wait for now, I will wait with You, because Your promises are true and Your aim and Your timing are perfect.

In the name of Jesus, amen.

I know the plans that I have for you, declares the LORD. They are plans for peace and not disaster, plans to give you a future filled with hope.

Jeremiah 29:11 GW

We know that God makes all things work together for the good of those who love Him and are chosen to be a part of His plan.

Romans 8:28 NLV

Wait patiently for the LORD.
Be brave and courageous.
Yes, wait patiently for the LORD.
Psalm 27:14 NLT

No one has ever heard,
no one has paid attention,
and no one has seen any god except you.
You help those who wait for you.
Isaiah 64:4 GW

The vision will still happen at the appointed time.
It hurries toward its goal.
It won't be a lie.
If it's delayed, wait for it.
It will certainly happen.
It won't be late.

Habakkuk 2:3 GW

Discouraged

Dear Lord,

Why does life have to be so hard that I begin to lose heart?

Maybe discouragement is the sign that I need to put my hope in You. When discouragement calls my name, I will look up and call *Your* name, for You are my rock. You have a higher perspective than I do, so I will look to You for guidance to find ways through my problems.

When I consider my problems, I think, *There's no way around this.* And maybe that's true—at least, there is no way without You. You have called me to live into the impossible, not through what I can figure out on my own but through You, through my faith in You.

I declare that I will not grow weary of doing the good You have called me to do but will continue to answer Your call through Your power. I will reap blessings by continuing onward and by not giving up.

You, O Lord, will lead me down paths I cannot see. You will guide me through the darkness. You will turn on Your light to illuminate my way. You will remove every obstacle so I will not stumble. You will do all these things for me, and You will never forsake me.

Why then should I take my eyes off You? You are the way through discouragement. I will look up and put my hope in You.

In the name of Jesus, amen.

From the ends of the earth, I call to you
    when I begin to lose heart.
Lead me to the rock that is high above me.

Psalm 61:2 GW

Our life is lived by faith. We do not live by what we see in front of us.

2 Corinthians 5:7 NLV

So let's not get tired of doing what is good. At just the right time we will reap a harvest of blessing if we don't give up.

Galatians 6:9 NLT

And I will lead the blind
    in a way that they do not know,
in paths that they have not known
    I will guide them.
I will turn the darkness before them into light,
    the rough places into level ground.
These are the things I do,
    and I do not forsake them.

Isaiah 42:16 ESV

Disillusioned

Dear Lord,

Be my light during times of confusion and darkness so that I do not become disillusioned, bending Your truth to suit lies or even my own will or desires.

May I not confuse Your light with darkness. May there be no dark corners within me so that I will glow with Your love, radiant, as though Your very presence has turned me into a floodlight.

In these last days, people will be deceived, loving themselves instead of loving You. They will worship money instead of worshiping You. They will be boastful, proud, and abusive and will disregard their parents' advice or warnings and behave and think like their peers.

May I not follow this way or be ungrateful, unholy, lacking in love, unforgiving, slanderous, lacking self-control, brutal, despising what's good, treacherous, rash, conceited, or a seeker of pleasure instead of a seeker of You.

But most of all, help me not to deceive myself by being a pretender, looking godly without having Your presence and power in my life. Empower me with more of Your Holy Spirit.

Before I belonged to You, I was full of darkness, but now I have Your light to show me the way to go. Help me to live my life as a person filled with Your light so that I can love others and know the difference between right and wrong as I determine how to live in a way that pleases You. May the light of Your love determine my every step.

In the name of Jesus, amen.

Make sure that the light you think you have is not actually darkness. If you are filled with light, with no dark corners, then your whole life will be radiant, as though a floodlight were filling you with light.

Luke 11:35–36 NLT

But mark this: There will be terrible times in the last days. People will be lovers of themselves, lovers of money, boastful, proud, abusive, disobedient to their parents, ungrateful, unholy, without love, unforgiving, slanderous, without self-control, brutal, not lovers of the good, treacherous, rash, conceited, lovers of pleasure rather than lovers of God—having a form of godliness but denying its power. Have nothing to do with such people.

2 Timothy 3:1–5 NIV

For once you were full of darkness, but now you have light from the Lord. So live as people of light! For this light within you produces only what is good and right and true. Carefully determine what pleases the Lord.

Ephesians 5:8–10 NLT

Distressed

Dear Lord,
     Whom can I call on when I'm in distress? Who will answer me?

You and only You. You answer my every call because nothing can separate me from Your love—not trouble, distress, persecution, hunger, nakedness, or danger. Not even a violent death can remove Your love from me.

You are always with me, always loving me, always giving me the gift of peace of mind and heart. Even if I had millions of dollars to spend, I would not be able to purchase this kind of peace.

When I am distressed, I will open my heart to receive Your gift of peace. I do so right now, casting out all my fear and replacing it with Your vibrant love for me. Because I have Your love, I have Your peace. I will not be troubled or afraid.

You are my shepherd, and I belong to You, which is why I am never in need. You make me to lie down in green pastures; You lead me beside peaceful waters. You renew my soul. You guide me along the paths of righteousness for the sake of Your name. Even when I walk through the dark valley of death, You are with me, and I will fear no harm.

Your authority over my life gives me courage. I lay all my distress at Your feet. I am Yours, and You are watching over me. Thank You!

In the name of Jesus, amen.

When I am in distress, I call to you,
    because you answer me.

Psalm 86:7 NIV

What will separate us from the love Christ has for us? Can trouble, distress, persecution, hunger, nakedness, danger, or violent death separate us from his love?

Romans 8:35 GW

I am leaving you with a gift—peace of mind and heart. And the peace I give is a gift the world cannot give. So don't be troubled or afraid.

John 14:27 NLT

The Lord is my shepherd.
    I am never in need.
        He makes me lie down in green pastures.
        He leads me beside peaceful waters.
        He renews my soul.
        He guides me along the paths of righteousness
            for the sake of his name.
Even though I walk through the dark valley of death,
    because you are with me, I fear no harm.
        Your rod and your staff give me courage.

Psalm 23:1–4 GW

Doubtful

Dear Lord,

Sometimes I think of the father who came to You because his child was in trouble. Instead of seeking You with great faith, he sought a miracle based on the hope that You would pity him.

I'm often like that father. I see what You can do, but instead of it stretching my faith, I hope for Your pity because I simply don't believe You want to move on my behalf.

But You are asking me not just to hope You will move but to believe You will. As that father cried, "Lord, I have faith; help my weak faith to be stronger!" I too cry out for stronger faith. I cannot please You without it.

When I go to You in prayer, help me to remember that You love me and that I am worthy in You. Help me to know that Your presence is with me and that You help my desires to line up with Your will as I seek You. You will give me greater faith so that I can be assured of things I expect and convinced of the existence of that which is not yet visible.

Help me to have eyes of faith so that I can see into the invisible and know that what I pray for is already mine.

I firmly declare that I believe in You and therefore believe that all things are possible because this is Your promise to me. You are forever faithful.

I come to You in greater faith now.

In the name of Jesus, amen.

"If You can do anything to help us, take pity on us!" Jesus said to him, "Why do you ask Me that? The one who has faith can do all things." At once the father cried out. He said with tears in his eyes, "Lord, I have faith. Help my weak faith to be stronger!"

Mark 9:22–24 NLV

No one can please God without faith. Whoever goes to God must believe that God exists and that he rewards those who seek him.

Hebrews 11:6 GW

Faith assures us of things we expect and convinces us of the existence of things we cannot see.

Hebrews 11:1 GW

That's why I tell you to have faith that you have already received whatever you pray for, and it will be yours.

Mark 11:24 GW

We must continue to hold firmly to our declaration of faith. The one who made the promise is faithful.

Hebrews 10:23 GW

Empty

Dear Lord,

There was a time I didn't have Your presence in my life. But in Your kindness and love for me, You saved me, not because I earned Your approval but because of Your great mercy toward me. You saved me by sending Your Son Jesus to take away my sin. You washed my sin away when I believed and gave my heart to You. You freed me of sin so that Your Holy Spirit could enter my soul and give me new birth and renewal.

So now, when I feel empty, I need to remember that I belong to You. I need to make sure I am right with You and that my spirit is a welcoming place for Your Spirit to dwell.

Create in me a clean heart, O God. Refresh me with Your Holy Spirit, for I want to stay with You and go where You lead me. Always refill me with Your presence and let the joy of Your saving grace restore me with Your power. Help me to have a willing spirit to obey You.

I don't want to copy the behavior and customs of this world. Lord, please transform me into the person You created me to be. Change my poor thinking and give me Your thoughts instead.

May I never be empty of Your presence, and may my hope grow stronger by the power of the Holy Spirit.

In the name of Jesus, amen.

Make a clean heart in me, O God. Give me a new spirit that will not be moved. Do not throw me away from where You are. And do not take Your Holy Spirit from me. Let the joy of Your saving power return to me. And give me a willing spirit to obey You.

Psalm 51:10–12 NLV

However, when God our Savior made his kindness and love for humanity appear, he saved us, but not because of anything we had done to gain his approval. Instead, because of his mercy he saved us through the washing in which the Holy Spirit gives us new birth and renewal.

Titus 3:4–5 GW

Don't copy the behavior and customs of this world, but let God transform you into a new person by changing the way you think.

Romans 12:2 NLT

May your hope grow stronger by the power of the Holy Spirit.

Romans 15:13 NLV

Exhausted

Dear Lord,

I've lived through stress, fought great battles, and swam through oceans of heartache, and now I am exhausted. As I look at the journey still before me, I wonder how I can take even one more step.

But you remind me that I don't have to continue this journey in my own strength. Because the heavier my load, the more I can carry in *Your* strength. When I find myself struggling, that is my cue to let go and rest in You. You even ask me to trade my burdens for You. You Yourself are never a burden because You are gentle and humble. When I'm yoked with You, the going is easy and my burden is light because Your strength replaces my weakness. Your power ignites my strength.

You are the eternal God, the Lord, the Creator of the ends of the earth. You never grow tired or become weary. Your understanding is beyond my ability to comprehend. You give me Your strength when I am tired. When everyone around me faints and falls left and right, You give me the wings of eagles so I can fly. Through You, I will run with fresh strength; I will walk without stumbling.

You lend me Your might so I do not need to fret or even consider giving up. For I can do all things through Christ who strengthens me.

In the name of Jesus, amen.

Come to me, all who are tired from carrying heavy loads, and I will give you rest. Place my yoke over your shoulders, and learn from me, because I am gentle and humble. Then you will find rest for yourselves because my yoke is easy and my burden is light.

Matthew 11:28–30 GW

Don't you know?
    Haven't you heard?
The eternal God, the LORD, the Creator of the ends
     of the earth,
    doesn't grow tired or become weary.
     His understanding is beyond reach.
He gives strength to those who grow tired
    and increases the strength of those who are weak.
Even young people grow tired and become weary,
    and young men will stumble and fall.
Yet, the strength of those who wait with hope in the
    LORD will be renewed.
    They will soar on wings like eagles.
     They will run and won't become weary.
     They will walk and won't grow tired.

Isaiah 40:28–31 GW

For I will help the tired ones and give strength to everyone who is weak.

Jeremiah 31:25 NLV

I can do everything through Christ who strengthens me.

Philippians 4:13 GW

Faith

Dear Lord,

I am so glad I heard about You. Because I believed what I heard, You rescued me from the kingdom of darkness. You redeemed me to Yourself because You wanted a relationship with me.

I cannot take credit for Your gift of salvation. It is a beautiful gift, not a reward for good behavior. I say yes to this gift as I boast in You and Your love.

Besides the gift of "salvation faith," You have also given me "the shield of faith" so I can protect myself from this world's dark rulers. The shield of faith is a gift I can wear when I wear Jesus Christ, the author and finisher of my faith.

You continue to shower me with gifts as I walk with You. You give me the gift of possibilities as I bring my prayer requests to You. For Jesus said, "But nothing is impossible with God."

I believe, Lord. I believe You are the one true God who sent His Son to die in my place. I believe You have forgiven me of my sins. I believe Your presence rests on me. I believe I can now walk and talk with You. I believe I can wear Your shield of faith to protect me from the evil one. You have given me faith to believe that all things are possible in You. You are the God of the impossible, and I am the proof.

In the name of Jesus, amen.

So faith comes from hearing, and hearing through the word of Christ.

Romans 10:17 ESV

God saved you by his grace when you believed. And you can't take credit for this; it is a gift from God. Salvation is not a reward for the good things we have done, so none of us can boast about it.

Ephesians 2:8–9 NLT

In addition to all this, take up the shield of faith, with which you can extinguish all the flaming arrows of the evil one.

Ephesians 6:16 NIV

Jesus said to him, "As far as possibilities go, everything is possible for the person who believes."

Mark 9:23 GW

But nothing is impossible for God.

Luke 1:37 GW

Fear

Dear Lord,
Help! I am afraid!

But I know that everything is okay because You've heard my cry and You will answer me. You never give me a spirit of fear but You give me a spirit of power and love and a good, sound mind.

When I stop to think about Your love for me, I am amazed. Your love indwells me. Your perfect love dissolves my fears, even when I don't recognize Your presence.

Even though I know I am not worthy of Your love, I do not fear that You will ever abandon or turn Your back on me. Your love is not based on my successes or my mistakes. You have a marvelous ability to love me despite my flaws.

Not only do You love me, but I belong to You. I only slip into fear when I forget whose I am. In those moments, I will choose to trust in You. I will praise You and marvel at Your Word. I will delight in the fact that nothing can destroy Your love for me. Nothing can destroy my soul, for it belongs to You.

Jesus promised after His death and resurrection that He would give me a gift: peace of mind and heart. That gift belongs to me. The world can never duplicate it or take it away. Because I claim this gift, I will not be troubled or afraid.

In the name of Jesus, amen.

I looked for the Lord, and He answered me. And He took away all my fears.

Psalm 34:4 NLV

For God did not give us a spirit of fear. He gave us a spirit of power and of love and of a good mind.

2 Timothy 1:7 NLV

There is no fear in love. Perfect love puts fear out of our hearts. People have fear when they are afraid of being punished. The man who is afraid does not have perfect love.

1 John 4:18 NLV

Even when I am afraid, I still trust you.
I praise God's word.
I trust God.
I am not afraid.
What can mere flesh and blood do to me?
Psalm 56:3–4 GW

I am leaving you with a gift—peace of mind and heart. And the peace I give is a gift the world cannot give. So don't be troubled or afraid.

John 14:27 NLT

Foolish

Dear Lord,

You are the inventor of wisdom, and those who reject You are foolish. They think themselves wise, but their own rebellious spirits have blinded them. They want only to serve their own selfish ambitions. They ignore You and plot against others, only to be caught in their own deceitful traps.

Help me to avoid those who run around like idiots trying to do as the world does. Their mad race leads to death. However, real wisdom can be found whenever I turn to You.

Thank You for being there for me. Remain in me as I remain in You. Give me the wisdom I need when I rub shoulders with those who walk the way the world walks. I know I am like a lamb among wolves, so help me to be as cunning as a snake yet as innocent as a dove.

Teach me Your ways so I will be wise. Help me to select wise friends and to be careful how I live, where I go, and what I do. Show me the truths I need. You are so generous with me, even giving me the wisdom to recognize my own folly. You never mock me but lovingly help me.

I pray that You, the Father of my Lord Jesus Christ, will give me a spirit of wisdom and revelation as I grow in my relationship with Christ.

In the name of Jesus, amen.

The wisdom of this rebellious and broken world looks like foolishness when put next to God. So it stands in Scripture, "He catches the wise in their deceitful plotting."

1 Corinthians 3:19 VOICE

So be careful how you live; be mindful of your steps. Don't run around like idiots as the rest of the world does. Instead, walk as the wise!

Ephesians 5:15 VOICE

I'm sending you out like sheep among wolves. So be as cunning as snakes but as innocent as doves.

Matthew 10:16 GW

If any of you needs wisdom to know what you should do, you should ask God, and he will give it to you. God is generous to everyone and doesn't find fault with them.

James 1:5 GW

I pray that the glorious Father, the God of our Lord Jesus Christ, would give you a spirit of wisdom and revelation as you come to know Christ better.

Ephesians 1:17 GW

Free

Dear Lord,

My enemy, that old thief, comes only to steal, kill, and destroy me. But You, Jesus, came to free me from his hand. You came so that I may have life and have it abundantly.

I cannot be captured by the evil one because my heart is free. My heart is free because my heart is where the Spirit of the Lord dwells. The Spirit of the Lord dwells in my heart because I believe that Jesus is the Son of God who has risen from the dead and has forgiven me of my sins. Because I believe and have been made new in Christ, the Spirit of the Lord rests His presence on me.

How glad I am that I have found this truth and that this truth has set me free not only from the enemy's grasp but also from sin and death.

I will celebrate my freedom by living free. Help me, Lord, not to use my freedom as a screen to hide behind when I do evil. Prick my heart so I might change my ways because I want to use my freedom to serve You.

Christ has freed me so that I can enjoy the freedom He gave me. I will enjoy it, and I will be firm in this freedom so that I will not become a slave again.

Reveal the enemy's traps and keep me free.

In the name of Jesus, amen.

The thief comes only to steal and kill and destroy. I came that they may have life and have it abundantly.

John 10:10 ESV

The heart is free where the Spirit of the Lord is. The Lord is the Spirit.

2 Corinthians 3:17 NLV

You will know the truth, and the truth will set you free.

John 8:32 GW

Live as free people, but don't hide behind your freedom when you do evil. Instead, use your freedom to serve God.

1 Peter 2:16 GW

Christ has freed us so that we may enjoy the benefits of freedom. Therefore, be firm in this freedom, and don't become slaves again.

Galatians 5:1 GW

Give Up

Dear Lord,

When I feel like giving up, I wonder if my race even matters.

What if my discouragement is nothing but lies from the enemy who wants to stop me in my tracks?

The reality is I'm not running this race by myself. I'm running it with You, my Lord and Savior. As I continue my race, You counter the enemy's lies with truth. You say, "Be strong. Do not give up." You promise that my efforts will be rewarded. As I look toward the finish line, I see Your smile and I know You are giving me the strength to run!

But I cannot run this race with a double mind. Help me to toss away everything that slows me down, especially the sin that has distracted me. Help me to keep my focus on You. You are both my source of strength and my goal. You ran Your race, You endured Your death on the cross, and You did it so that one day I can run into Your arms. What joy we will share! Because You endured so much for me, I will endure my race for You. Give me the strength to never give up.

I will be strong and courageous! I will not be afraid or discouraged. Your love is my strength, and You are with me as I run. You will be with me when I cross the finish line.

In the name of Jesus, amen.

But as for you, be strong and do not give up, for your work will be rewarded.

2 Chronicles 15:7 NIV

Since we are surrounded by so many examples of faith, we must get rid of everything that slows us down, especially sin that distracts us. We must run the race that lies ahead of us and never give up. We must focus on Jesus, the source and goal of our faith. He saw the joy ahead of him, so he endured death on the cross and ignored the disgrace it brought him. Now he holds the honored position—the one next to God the Father on the heavenly throne. Think about Jesus, who endured opposition from sinners, so that you don't become tired and give up.

Hebrews 12:1–3 GW

This is my command—be strong and courageous! Do not be afraid or discouraged. For the LORD your God is with you wherever you go.

Joshua 1:9 NLT

God's Presence

ear Lord,

Just as Moses didn't want to journey to the promised land without You, neither do I.

When Moses complained about the crowd of stiff-necked people You called him to lead, You comforted him and told him that Your presence would go with him and that You would give him peace.

I too ask for Your presence and peace to go with me. Please!

It is good to be near You, Lord. No matter my crazy schedule, work politics, family dynamics, or the drama in my life, You are my safe place. I seek Your shelter and tell of all the wondrous things You have done.

I seek You because I am Your child. You have given me Your Holy Spirit. Your Spirit is inside me and calls back to You, "My dear Father!"

I am much like Your holy temple, for just as Your Spirit rested in the Holy of Holies, Your Holy Spirit rests in my heart. Because Your Spirit is alive inside me and because my salvation came at a great price, I must honor You with my body.

May Your Spirit always rest inside me, giving me peace, love, joy, and strength in my weakness. Your Spirit even intercedes for me when I don't know what to pray.

Help me to make my heart a wonderful home for Your presence. Fill me to the brim.

In the name of Jesus, amen.

The LORD answered, "My presence will go with you, and I will give you peace."

Exodus 33:14 GW

But as for me, it is good to be near God. I have made the Lord God my safe place. So I may tell of all the things You have done.

Psalm 73:28 NLV

Because you are God's children, God has sent the Spirit of his Son into us to call out, "Abba Father!"

Galatians 4:6 GW

Do you not know that your bodies are temples of the Holy Spirit, who is in you, whom you have received from God? You are not your own; you were bought at a price. Therefore honor God with your bodies.

1 Corinthians 6:19–20 NIV

At the same time the Spirit also helps us in our weakness, because we don't know how to pray for what we need. But the Spirit intercedes along with our groans that cannot be expressed in words.

Romans 8:26 GW

Grace

Dear Lord,

Thank You for the grace You have so generously given me, not because I have achieved perfection, but simply because I am Your child.

It is by grace I have been saved, through faith. This is not something I did for myself, and I in no way deserve it. Your grace is a gift that You have given to me because of Your kindness and generosity. I cannot boast in myself; I can boast only in You.

Because of Your saving grace, sin is no longer my master. I no longer have to live a perfect life under the law, a law that demanded constant animal sacrifices for every sin. When Jesus became my once-and-for-all sacrifice for sin, I was set free from the law. This is why I can live in Your freedom.

Your grace is sufficient for me, and Your power is made perfect in my weakness. I can't live this life of grace by myself; I can live it only in and through You. Therefore, I will boast in how You turn my weaknesses into strength through the mighty power of Christ.

I humbly draw near to You. I approach Your throne of grace with confidence so that I may receive more grace to help me in my time of need.

May I live my life in Your grace so I can share it with others.

In the name of Jesus, amen.

And he gives grace generously. As the Scriptures say,

> "God opposes the proud
> but gives grace to the humble."

James 4:6 NLT

For it is by grace you have been saved, through faith—and this is not from yourselves, it is the gift of God—not by works, so that no one can boast.

Ephesians 2:8–9 NIV

Sin is no longer your master, for you no longer live under the requirements of the law. Instead, you live under the freedom of God's grace.

Romans 6:14 NLT

But he said to me, "My grace is sufficient for you, for my power is made perfect in weakness." Therefore I will boast all the more gladly about my weaknesses, so that Christ's power may rest on me.

2 Corinthians 12:9 NIV

Let us then with confidence draw near to the throne of grace, that we may receive mercy and find grace to help in time of need.

Hebrews 4:16 ESV

Grief

Dear Lord,

You are so dear. You take care of me when I suffer, and You heal my broken heart. You are the one who bandages my wounds and loves me through my tears.

I praise You, God and Father of our Lord Jesus Christ! You are the Father who is compassionate to me, the God who comforts me. You carry me through the deep waters, even when I'm not aware You are holding me close. You comfort me when I hurt. Because I have experienced Your comfort, I can share Your comfort with others. It's a personal gift from You to me, a gift I can share as often as needed.

You bless me when I weep, for my tears will not last forever, and You will once again restore me to laughter. You are close to me when my heart is broken; You rescue me when I am crushed.

This old earth is not yet heaven, but some day, when You call me home, You will wipe away every tear from my eyes. There will be no more death or sorrow or crying or pain. All these things will be gone forever.

And I will be with You, my joy restored, my peace complete. What a day that will be!

For now, I ask You to hold me close as I lay my grief at Your feet. Remind me of Your love, and help me to see Your goodness in the land of the living.

In the name of Jesus, amen.

He is the healer of the brokenhearted.
He is the one who bandages their wounds.

Psalm 147:3 GW

Praise the God and Father of our Lord Jesus Christ! He is the Father who is compassionate and the God who gives comfort. He comforts us whenever we suffer. That is why whenever other people suffer, we are able to comfort them by using the same comfort we have received from God.

2 Corinthians 1:3–4 GW

God blesses you who weep now,
for in due time you will laugh.

Luke 6:21 NLT

The LORD is close to the brokenhearted;
he rescues those whose spirits are crushed.

Psalm 34:18 NLT

He will wipe every tear from their eyes, and there will be no more death or sorrow or crying or pain. All these things are gone forever.

Revelation 21:4 NLT

Guilt

Dear Lord,

It's a wonder to think that seven hundred years before Jesus was born, You told Your prophet Isaiah that even though our sins are bright red, they will become as white as snow, as white as wool.

Your Son Jesus fulfilled this prophecy when You sent Him into the world, not to condemn it, but to save it. Jesus became the sacrifice for my sin by dying a terrible death on the cross, where He *became* my sin. He took my sin and gave me His righteousness so that I can have the privilege to be covered in His holiness and to walk with You.

Lord, You are faithful and reliable, and my sin no longer separates me from You. When I confess my sins to You, You forgive them, and You cleanse me from everything I've done wrong.

In that moment, the Holy Spirit touches my soul, and I become a dwelling place for Him. My old life is gone; my new life has begun.

I confess now that Jesus is Lord, and I cast my sin on Him in exchange for His righteousness. I turn from my sin and invite the presence of Your Spirit to rest in my heart as I become a new person.

Lord, help me to keep our relationship vibrant by remembering to come to You for renewal. Remind me that I am under Your grace. Help me to walk holy and blameless in and with You.

In the name of Jesus, amen.

"Come on now, let's discuss this!" says the LORD.
"Though your sins are bright red,
   they will become as white as snow.
Though they are dark red,
   they will become as white as wool."

Isaiah 1:18 GW

For God did not send his Son into the world to condemn the world, but to save the world through him.

John 3:17 NIV

God made him who had no sin to be sin for us, so that in him we might become the righteousness of God.

2 Corinthians 5:21 NIV

God is faithful and reliable. If we confess our sins, he forgives them and cleanses us from everything we've done wrong.

1 John 1:9 GW

For if a man belongs to Christ, he is a new person. The old life is gone. New life has begun.

2 Corinthians 5:17 NLV

Harassed

Dear Lord,

The devil is alive and well and on the prowl. As I grow in You and follow Your will, he tries to shoot missiles of distraction my way. But I will not fear, because I place myself under Your protection and authority as I trust in You. I resist the enemy in the name of Jesus, and as I do, he flees!

How I love that I can come to You when he harasses me. Not only will You turn his harassments into blessings, but You will also protect me.

To paraphrase the words of Moses in Psalm 91:

I live under Your shelter and hide in Your shadow. I say to You, "You are my safe place and my fortress. You are the one I trust. You rescue me from the enemy's traps and plagues. You cover me in Your feathers. I will find refuge beneath Your wing. Your truth is my shield and armor. Because of You, I do not fear terrors of the night, arrows that fly in the day, plagues that roam the dark, or epidemics that strike in the light of day. They will not come near me. Even if thousands fall around me, I will be safe. You punish the guilty, but I am counted innocent."

I will not open the door to the enemy with wrongdoing. Instead, I will slam the door shut and follow You, Lord, with all my heart.

In the name of Jesus, amen.

So place yourselves under God's authority. Resist the devil, and he will run away from you.

James 4:7 GW

> Whoever lives under the shelter of the Most High
> will remain in the shadow of the Almighty.
> I will say to the LORD,
> "You are my refuge and my fortress, my God in
> whom I trust."
> He is the one who will rescue you from hunters' traps
> and from deadly plagues.
> He will cover you with his feathers,
> and under his wings you will find refuge.
> His truth is your shield and armor.
> You do not need to fear
> terrors of the night,
> arrows that fly during the day,
> plagues that roam the dark,
> epidemics that strike at noon.
> They will not come near you,
> even though a thousand may fall dead beside
> you or ten thousand at your right side.
> You only have to look with your eyes
> to see the punishment of wicked people.

Psalm 91:1–8 GW

Don't give the devil any opportunity to work.

Ephesians 4:27 GW

Hate

Dear Lord,

You call me to hate what is sinful, so I hate pride, arrogance, and lying, especially when these sins are found in me.

But even though You call me to hate sin, You also call me to love sinners. You want me to love my neighbors, including the difficult people You have placed into my life. You ask me to cover wrongs with love instead of allowing wrongs or disagreements to pull me into foolish quarrels. You show me how blind I am when I refuse to forgive my brother. You teach me that hate plunges me into darkness instead of allowing me to stay in Your light.

You are delighted when I lay down my pride and forgo the right to be proven right. You are pleased when I love those who don't deserve my love. After all, I don't deserve Your love either.

So, Lord, I open my heart to receive more of Your love so that I can love everyone in my life—through Your power. I bless those who curse me and pray they will turn their hearts to You.

Lord, the world may hate me, but it hated You first. Just as You chose me to be in Your kingdom, I choose to follow You instead of following the world.

It is my prayer, Lord, that as I love others, they will feel Your love through me. Please give them the opportunity to discover how Your love can change their lives.

In the name of Jesus, amen.

The fear of the Lord is to hate what is sinful. I hate pride, self-love, the way of sin, and lies.

Proverbs 8:13 NLV

Hate starts quarrels,
but love covers every wrong.
Proverbs 10:12 GW

Whoever hates his brother is not in the light but lives in darkness. He does not know where he is going because the darkness has blinded his eyes.

1 John 2:11 NLV

But to you who are willing to listen, I say, love your enemies! Do good to those who hate you. Bless those who curse you. Pray for those who hurt you.

Luke 6:27–28 NLT

If the world hates you, realize that it hated me before it hated you. If you had anything in common with the world, the world would love you as one of its own. But you don't have anything in common with the world. I chose you from the world, and that's why the world hates you.

John 15:18–19 GW

Hope

Dear Lord,

I praise You, the God and Father of my Lord Jesus Christ!

How wonderful that Christ, in His great mercy, has given me new birth and a living hope through His resurrection from the dead. I now have the gift of not only walking with You but the joy of spending eternity with You.

Your unfailing love is with me. Even as I put my hope in You, I know that my hope is also your gift to me. You continue to fill me with joy and peace as I trust in You. Help me to trust You more so that my joy and peace may increase. Help my hope to grow even stronger by the power of the Holy Spirit.

You, Lord, have not abandoned me to the wiles of this world. In fact, You have plans for me. Your plans include my well-being, not trouble. You want to give me a future and a hope.

How amazing that though this is not heaven, You are making a way for me to thrive with purpose. Lead me to Your purpose every day of my life.

I love You, Lord, and I thank You for renewing my strength. I will soar on wings like eagles, I will run and not grow weary, I will walk and not faint.

When I look to You, the darkness flees and hope lights my way.

In the name of Jesus, amen.

Praise be to the God and Father of our Lord Jesus Christ! In his great mercy he has given us new birth into a living hope through the resurrection of Jesus Christ from the dead.

1 Peter 1:3 NIV

May your unfailing love be with us, LORD,
even as we put our hope in you.

Psalm 33:22 NIV

Our hope comes from God. May He fill you with joy and peace because of your trust in Him. May your hope grow stronger by the power of the Holy Spirit.

Romans 15:13 NLV

"For I know the plans I have for you," says the Lord, "plans for well-being and not for trouble, to give you a future and a hope."

Jeremiah 29:11 NLV

But those who hope in the LORD
will renew their strength.
They will soar on wings like eagles;
they will run and not grow weary,
they will walk and not be faint.

Isaiah 40:31 NIV

Hurt

Dear Lord,

What is Your remedy for hurt feelings, wounded pride, unjust treatment, and smashed toes? I want to know because I'm hurting and I have a few scars that remind me of the wrongs committed against me. Just when I come up with the perfect retort, You whisper to my heart that I should love my enemies. You even suggest I pray for those who torment and persecute me—because I belong to You.

I was throwing a pity party, but when I invited You, You asked me to lay down my offenses and forgive those who hurt me, just as You have forgiven me.

You are telling me it's not my place to take revenge. You want me to leave my complaints in Your hands because Scripture reminds me that if I don't make the mistake of taking justice into my own hands, You will act in my behalf.

It's hard to bear the pain of my wounds, until I remember that You will fight for me. All I have to do is stay calm.

Watch over me, Lord, and make sure I don't miss the revelation of Your grace. Help me to uproot bitterness so that my heart will not be full of poison. Fill my heart instead with Your love so that I can heal and overcome my wounds and love those who wounded me.

In the name of Jesus, amen.

But I tell you this: love your enemies. Pray for those who torment you and persecute you—in so doing, you become children of your Father in heaven.

Matthew 5:44–45 VOICE

Put up with each other, and forgive each other if anyone has a complaint. Forgive as the Lord forgave you.

Colossians 3:13 GW

Beloved, don't be obsessed with taking revenge, but leave that to God's righteous justice. For the Scriptures say:

"If you don't take justice in your own hands,
I will release justice for you," says the Lord.

Romans 12:19 TPT

The Lord himself will fight for you. Just stay calm.

Exodus 14:14 NLT

Watch over each other to make sure that no one misses the revelation of God's grace. And make sure no one lives with a root of bitterness sprouting within them which will only cause trouble and poison the hearts of many.

Hebrews 12:15 TPT

Impatience

Dear Lord,

It's hard to be patient. It's hard to look forward to something I'm waiting to have or hope will happen. But patience is how You call me to live. You call me to practice patience with confidence.

As I wait, I learn to trust You more. Trusting You gives me the strength to be brave and courageous because what I am really waiting for is You. I don't need to worry because I know Your timing is perfect, and even when You wait till the last minute, You are always on time.

Help me to be still in Your presence and to experience Your peace as I wait for You to move. As I wait, I have no need to worry about evil people who prosper; neither do I need to fret about their wicked schemes.

I wait in confidence of Your love for me. As I experience Your love, I begin to see that love itself is patient and kind. It is never jealous, and it never sings its own praises because it isn't arrogant. I will wait in Your love, knowing that You are not tormenting me but strengthening me.

As I wait, I will answer Your call to do good. Help me to put on Your patience so I do not tire from acts of kindness. You will harvest the good I've planted when I don't give up and quit.

In the name of Jesus, amen.

But if we look forward to something we don't yet have, we must wait patiently and confidently.

Romans 8:25 NLT

> Wait patiently for the LORD.
>> Be brave and courageous.
>> Yes, wait patiently for the LORD.
>>> Psalm 27:14 NLT

> Be still in the presence of the LORD,
>> and wait patiently for him to act.
> Don't worry about evil people who prosper
>> or fret about their wicked schemes.
>>> Psalm 37:7 NLT

Love is patient. Love is kind. Love isn't jealous. It doesn't sing its own praises. It isn't arrogant.

1 Corinthians 13:4 GW

So let's not allow ourselves to get fatigued doing good. At the right time we will harvest a good crop if we don't give up, or quit. Right now, therefore, every time we get the chance, let us work for the benefit of all, starting with the people closest to us in the community of faith.

Galatians 6:9–10 MSG

Jealous

Dear Lord,

You ask me to guard my heart so that I will be true to You. You ask that I not worship other gods, including my own selfishness. You ask this of me not because You are controlling but because You are trying to protect me from the destructive power of false gods birthed from my selfishness, misjudgments, or folly.

When my head is turned to other gods, including wealth, status, and power, bitterness creeps into my life. This root of bitterness comes from being jealous of others, and jealousy has the destructive power to rot my bones. Jealousy causes selfish ambitions powered not by the Holy Spirit but by the demonic powers of this world. Envy can cause disorder and results in vile practices. It is even more dangerous than cruel anger.

Help me to serve You alone and to have a heart of peace that gives life to my body. Help me to do nothing out of jealousy but instead to base my actions on love. Love never gives up. Love is kind. Love is not jealous. Love does not put itself up as being important. Love has no pride.

Lord, forgive me of my jealousy. I repent and turn away from such dangerous business. Restore my heart to love, and set me free from my selfish ambitions as I determine to trust You with my life.

In the name of Jesus, amen.

Do not worship any other god, for the LORD, whose name is Jealous, is a jealous God.

Exodus 34:14 NIV

A heart at peace gives life to the body,
but envy rots the bones.

Proverbs 14:30 NIV

But if you have bitter jealousy and selfish ambition in your hearts, do not boast and be false to the truth. This is not the wisdom that comes down from above, but is earthly, unspiritual, demonic. For where jealousy and selfish ambition exist, there will be disorder and every vile practice.

James 3:14–16 ESV

Anger is cruel, and wrath is like a flood,
but jealousy is even more dangerous.

Proverbs 27:4 NLT

Love does not give up. Love is kind. Love is not jealous. Love does not put itself up as being important. Love has no pride.

1 Corinthians 13:4 NLV

Joy

Dear Lord,

When my anxiety builds, it's time to trust You more. When I do so, You replace my anxiety with joy, and my mood remarkably improves.

Help me to remain joyful as I continually reach out to You in prayer, thanking You for all the good things You give to me. When I remember to count my blessings, I am counted blessed.

No matter what happens, I have learned that I can count it all joy, even when I am in the midst of difficult trials; for trials help test my faith. These faith tests teach me how to remain steadfast in my relationship with You, and by remaining steadfast, I am made perfect and complete in You, lacking nothing.

As I follow after joy, I will make room for more of Your Holy Spirit's presence in my life, for the Spirit's presence gives me more love, joy, peace, patience, kindness, goodness, faithfulness, gentleness, and self-control, traits no one can condemn.

Lord, You love me and show me the way to live. You bring me joy. You give me happiness forevermore.

I have decided to count this day as joyful, for this is the day you have made for me to share with You, which is all the more reason to rejoice and be glad.

In the name of Jesus, amen.

When anxiety was great within me,
your consolation brought me joy.

Psalm 94:19 NIV

Always be joyful. Never stop praying. Whatever happens, give thanks, because it is God's will in Christ Jesus that you do this.

1 Thessalonians 5:16–18 GW

Count it all joy, my brothers, when you meet trials of various kinds, for you know that the testing of your faith produces steadfastness. And let steadfastness have its full effect, that you may be perfect and complete, lacking in nothing.

James 1:2–4 ESV

But the Holy Spirit produces this kind of fruit in our lives: love, joy, peace, patience, kindness, goodness, faithfulness, gentleness, and self-control. There is no law against these things!

Galatians 5:22–23 NLT

You will show me the way of life. Being with You is to be full of joy. In Your right hand there is happiness forever.

Psalm 16:11 NLV

This is the day the Lord has made.
Let's rejoice and be glad today!

Psalm 118:24 GW

Lonely

Dear Lord,

In the times I feel most alone, I remember that You are with me. You have promised that You will never leave me. Because You are here, You hear my cries for help. You encourage me through my loneliness, reminding me of your presence.

I know You are with me because Your Holy Spirit lives inside of me. This truth gives me the confidence to know that I belong to You.

Not only are You with me, You promise to help by leading me out of trouble.

Even when I lose those I love to death and feel the loneliness of their absence, You are near. You are there to walk with me through this dark valley. You are there to carry me through my grief. You protect me from harm with Your rod and staff. You honor me in front of my enemies, and You anoint me with Your loving presence so that my cup overflows.

When the enemy tells me that You have abandoned me, help me to recognize his words are lies! May the sound of those lies signal me to reach out to You, the one who loves me. Your presence will shatter his lies because You are always by my side, even unto the end of time.

You always hear my cry because You are near, and nearer still. Thank You that You will never abandon me. My cup overflows with gratitude.

In the name of Jesus, amen.

You, however, are not in the realm of the flesh but are in the realm of the Spirit, if indeed the Spirit of God lives in you. And if anyone does not have the Spirit of Christ, they do not belong to Christ.

Romans 8:9 NIV

Even though I walk through the dark valley of death,
because you are with me, I fear no harm.
Your rod and your staff give me courage.
You prepare a banquet for me while my enemies watch.
You anoint my head with oil.
My cup overflows.

Psalm 23:4–5 GW

And remember that I am always with you until the end of time.

Matthew 28:20 GW

God has said, "I will never abandon you or leave you." So we can confidently say,

"The Lord is my helper.
I will not be afraid."

Hebrews 13:5–6 GW

Loss

Dear Lord,

Though the shock of my loss breaks my heart, You are the God who comforts me and heals my shattered spirit. I come to You, crying out with all my heart, and You hear and rescue me. You draw near when I am crushed with pain. You use Your miraculous power to restore my life. When bad things happen to me or to those I love, You save me and will not allow me to be defeated.

This is not yet heaven, but one day when You call me to Yourself in the eternal, You will wipe every tear from my eyes, and loss will be no more. There will be no cancer, illness, divorce, unemployment, rejection, betrayal, difficulties, death, sorrow, tears, pandemic, or pain. They will not exist.

My loss is not a sign that You have turned from me. In fact, You hold me close. You have heard my cry and have not hidden Your face from me.

Lord, I open my broken heart to You. Restore me so that I can feel Your grace, love, and comfort. Take me through this valley with a song of praise on my lips, for I know that You are not the author of my pain. It is the enemy who steals, kills, and destroys, not You. You are my healer, and I choose to trust You no matter what I face. You will use each valley to make me stronger and draw me closer.

In the name of Jesus, amen.

He heals the wounds of every shattered heart.

Psalm 147:3 TPT

Yet when holy lovers of God cry out
to him with all their hearts,
the Lord will hear them and come to rescue them
from all their troubles.
The Lord is close to all whose hearts are crushed by pain,
and he is always ready to restore the repentant one.
Even when bad things happen to the good and godly
    ones,
the Lord will save them and not let them be defeated
by what they face.

Psalm 34:17–19 TPT

He will wipe every tear from their eyes, and there will be no more death or sorrow or crying or pain. All these things are gone forever.

Revelation 21:4 NLT

For He has not turned away from the suffering of the one in pain or trouble. He has not hidden His face from him. But He has heard his cry for help.

Psalm 22:24 NLV

Love

Dear Lord,

Because of Your love for me, I love You and the people You have put in my life.

If I could speak all the languages of the earth and the languages of angels but didn't love others, my efforts would be nothing more than a clang of a bell.

If I had a supernatural gift of prophecy and understood all Your secret plans, if I possessed all knowledge, and if I had the faith to pray and see the mountains move but didn't love others, I would be of no value.

If I gave everything I have to the poor and even sacrificed my body but didn't love others, I could not boast because my sacrifice would have gained nothing.

Help me to be patient and kind and not jealous or rude, demanding my own way. Help me to love others more, for love never gives up. Love never loses faith and is always hopeful. Love endures through every circumstance.

Keep me aware of Your love so that I will not be irritable or keep a record of wrongs. When I have more of Your love, am aware of Your love, and learn to flow in Your love, I become like a river pouring from the throne of heaven, anointing others.

Help me to endure through every circumstance so that Your river of love will flow from Your heart to my heart, then from my heart to the world.

In the name of Jesus, amen.

If I could speak all the languages of earth and of angels, but didn't love others, I would only be a noisy gong or a clanging cymbal. If I had the gift of prophecy, and if I understood all of God's secret plans and possessed all knowledge, and if I had such faith that I could move mountains, but didn't love others, I would be nothing. If I gave everything I have to the poor and even sacrificed my body, I could boast about it; but if I didn't love others, I would have gained nothing.

Love is patient and kind. Love is not jealous or boastful or proud or rude. It does not demand its own way. It is not irritable, and it keeps no record of being wronged. It does not rejoice about injustice but rejoices whenever the truth wins out. Love never gives up, never loses faith, is always hopeful, and endures through every circumstance.

1 Corinthians 13:1–7 NLT

Lord, you're so kind and tenderhearted
to those who don't deserve it
and so patient with people who fail you!
Your love is like a flooding river
overflowing its banks with kindness.

Psalm 103:8 TPT

Lust

Dear Lord,

Sometimes I am tempted by my desires, desires that could lure me away from my holy walk with You. Help me not to fall into this trap, and forgive me when I do!

Help me to keep my thoughts on You and all that is good so that I don't flirt with sin and lose control. If I fail, then my desires could become pregnant and give birth to sin. And if my sin grows up, it could give birth to death.

I choose life not death, so I am asking You for Your help. Help me to stay away from the kinds of lusts that tempt me. Help me to pursue faith, love, and peace as I worship You with a pure heart.

Help me to yield freely and fully to the dynamic life and power of the Holy Spirit. Help me to abandon my cravings for sin and instead crave more of You. It is better to be filled with Your Spirit than to be full of myself.

It is Your will that I set myself apart and live a holy life, not polluting myself with sexual sin and defilement. Help me to take charge over my body and to maintain my purity and honor, because in this way I know that You will keep me free from lustful passions that could take over my life. I also break any spirit of lust that the enemy would try to use to trap me.

In the name of Jesus, amen.

Everyone is tempted by his own desires as they lure him away and trap him. Then desire becomes pregnant and gives birth to sin. When sin grows up, it gives birth to death.

James 1:14–15 GW

Stay away from lusts which tempt young people. Pursue what has God's approval. Pursue faith, love, and peace together with those who worship the Lord with a pure heart.

2 Timothy 2:22 GW

As you yield freely and fully to the dynamic life and power of the Holy Spirit, you will abandon the cravings of your self-life.

Galatians 5:16 TPT

Now this is God's will for you: set yourselves apart and live holy lives; avoid polluting yourselves with sexual defilement. Learn how to take charge over your own body, maintaining purity and honor. Don't let the swells of lustful passion run your life as they do the outsiders who don't know God.

1 Thessalonians 4:3–5 VOICE

Offended

Dear Lord,

When it comes to an offense, help me to have good sense. Give me wisdom to overlook it or even to break through it. But if the offense continues or builds, help me to keep my emotions in check so that anger does not rule my life, not even for a day. Friends, family members, my marriage, opportunities, and my job could be lost if I lose this battle.

Help me to keep the devil, that slanderous accuser, at bay so that he does not have a chance to use anger to manipulate me.

If things get to a point where I do need to react, help me to react in love. If another believer sins against me, lead me to go privately to that person and point out how they hurt me. If they listen and respond with understanding, I will still have my friend.

But if the meeting is unsuccessful, give me the courage and the wisdom to select a wise friend or two to return and discuss the matter with my offending friend.

If my friend still refuses to listen, be with me as I take the matter to the church. If this meeting fails to bring resolution, then allow me to walk away from the relationship.

Give me wisdom and love so that I can hear Your heart, especially if this is nothing more than a misunderstanding, confusion, or even a lie from the enemy. May Your love direct me to reconciliation.

In the name of Jesus, amen.

A person with good sense is patient,
and it is to his credit that he overlooks an offense.

Proverbs 19:11 GW

But don't let the passion of your emotions lead you to sin! Don't let anger control you or be fuel for revenge, not for even a day. Don't give the slanderous accuser, the Devil, an opportunity to manipulate you!

Ephesians 4:26–27 TPT

If another believer sins against you, go privately and point out the offense. If the other person listens and confesses it, you have won that person back. But if you are unsuccessful, take one or two others with you and go back again, so that everything you say may be confirmed by two or three witnesses. If the person still refuses to listen, take your case to the church. Then if he or she won't accept the church's decision, treat that person as a pagan or a corrupt tax collector.

Matthew 18:15–17 NLT

Oppressed

Dear Lord,

My enemy Satan roams the earth like a roaring lion looking for an easy meal. He lays traps to capture me; he spreads lies and tries to lure me into sin.

I cannot be naive, for my enemy is not flesh and blood but evil rulers and authorities, and mighty powers and evil spirits in the unseen world and heavenly places.

This is why I must wear the protection of the armor of God. Lord, I will put on Your armor so that I can stand firm as I stand against the strategies of the devil. I will put on Your armor so that I can resist the enemy and his attacks.

I will stand my ground, putting on the belt of truth, which will destroy the enemy's lies. I will wear the body armor of the righteousness of Jesus so that the enemy cannot accuse me. I will put on the shoes of peace, which comes from the Good News of Jesus Christ. I will hold up the shield of faith to stop the fiery arrows of the devil so that the enemy cannot hit his mark. I will put on the helmet of salvation given to me by Jesus and will take up the sword of the Spirit, the mighty Word of God. I will pray as the Spirit of God leads me. I will stay alert and pray for others as You put them on my heart.

In the name of Jesus, amen.

Stay alert! Watch out for your great enemy, the devil. He prowls around like a roaring lion, looking for someone to devour.

1 Peter 5:8 NLT

Put on all of God's armor so that you will be able to stand firm against all strategies of the devil. For we are not fighting against flesh-and-blood enemies, but against evil rulers and authorities of the unseen world, against mighty powers in this dark world, and against evil spirits in the heavenly places. Therefore, put on every piece of God's armor so you will be able to resist the enemy in the time of evil. Then after the battle you will still be standing firm. Stand your ground, putting on the belt of truth and the body armor of God's righteousness. For shoes, put on the peace that comes from the Good News so that you will be fully prepared. In addition to all of these, hold up the shield of faith to stop the fiery arrows of the devil. Put on salvation as your helmet, and take the sword of the Spirit, which is the word of God. Pray in the Spirit at all times and on every occasion. Stay alert and be persistent in your prayers for all believers everywhere.

Ephesians 6:11–18 NLT

Overwhelmed

Dear Lord,

You tell me to come to You when I am overwhelmed and weary from carrying heavy burdens. So here I am! I accept the rest that You offer me.

I no longer carry the weight of my burdens by myself. From this moment on, I will be yoked to You, and You will do all the heavy pulling and lifting. You offer to teach me with Your gentle heart and humble Spirit so that I can find rest for my soul. My response is yes! Yes, I want to draw even closer to You. Yes, I want to hear all that You have to say to me through the power of Your Word and Your precious Holy Spirit.

Because I am made new in You, I have already won the victory over the world through my faith in You.

I will not lose heart. Even though I continue to age on the outside, I remain young on the inside as Your Spirit renews me. My troubles are only light and temporary. You count my faithfulness through my troubles as a solid path to Your eternal glory.

Help me to keep my eyes on You, not on the things of this world. When I focus on You and Your kingdom, I see the eternal.

I will press on in Your power and through Your Spirit. I will not be overcome with fatigue for doing what is right. I will continue on in my journey, refreshed in You.

In the name of Jesus, amen.

Come to me, all of you who are weary and carry heavy burdens, and I will give you rest. Take my yoke upon you. Let me teach you, because I am humble and gentle at heart, and you will find rest for your souls.

Matthew 11:28–29 NLT

Everyone who has been born from God has won the victory over the world. Our faith is what wins the victory over the world.

1 John 5:4 GW

Therefore we do not lose heart. Though outwardly we are wasting away, yet inwardly we are being renewed day by day. For our light and momentary troubles are achieving for us an eternal glory that far outweighs them all. So we fix our eyes not on what is seen, but on what is unseen, since what is seen is temporary, but what is unseen is eternal.

2 Corinthians 4:16–18 NIV

We can't allow ourselves to get tired of doing what is right.

2 Thessalonians 3:13 GW

Pain

Dear Lord,

Thank You for loving me and for rescuing me. It's wonderful that You protect me because I know Your name.

You have promised that when I call on You, You will answer me. I invite You into my trouble, for I know that You will save and honor me. You will satisfy me with a long life.

Thank You for restoring my health and healing my wounds. When You heal me, I am healed. When You rescue me, I am rescued, and I praise Your name.

When I think about how the prophet Isaiah described Christ Jesus, seven centuries before Jesus was born of a virgin, I marvel. Isaiah foretold of how Jesus took my pain, bore my suffering, and was stricken, afflicted, and punished by God for my sin. Lord, You were pierced for my wrongdoings. You were crushed for my sinful failures. Your punishment brought me peace, and by Your wounds I am healed.

I give you my pain, and I ask that You heal me and show me Your good and perfect will so that I can have all the faith I need to believe. Help my unbelief.

But if You heal me now, or if my healing is gradual, or if You heal me when You call me home to heaven, I will trust You. I admit that I do not understand all Your ways, but I trust You and praise You.

I trust You now. I do believe. Thank You!

In the name of Jesus, amen.

Because you love me, I will rescue you.
I will protect you because you know my name.
When you call to me, I will answer you.
I will be with you when you are in trouble.
I will save you and honor you.
I will satisfy you with a long life.
I will show you how I will save you.

Psalm 91:14–16 GW

"I'll restore your health and heal your wounds," declares the Lord.

Jeremiah 30:17 GW

Heal me, O Lord, and I will be healed.
Rescue me, and I will be rescued.
You are the one I praise.

Jeremiah 17:14 GW

Surely he took up our pain
and bore our suffering,
yet we considered him punished by God,
stricken by him, and afflicted.
But he was pierced for our transgressions,
he was crushed for our iniquities;
the punishment that brought us peace was on him,
and by his wounds we are healed.

Isaiah 53:4–5 NIV

Peace

Dear Lord,

I need more of Your peace. In fact, I need more of Your peace not only in my soul but also in the relationships in my life. Please let me be a peacemaker, for Jesus taught that I am blessed when I make peace and I will be called a child of God.

Also, let me be a peace finder. I will find Your peace when I sharpen my focus on You. When I sharpen my focus, I see more of who You are and discover that You are a God I can trust. When I trust in You, You give me an endless supply of peace.

Teach me how to receive your gift of perfect peace. When I have Your perfect peace, I am able to keep my mind on you. Having more of your perfect peace means I can stop worrying. I will be able to pray about everything and look to You for answers. As I look to You, I will give thanks every time I ask You for what I need, for I know that You will answer; I know that You will take good care of me.

When my trust in You grows, my peace will be greater than I can understand. Your peace will keep my heart and mind through Jesus Christ.

Lord, please give me peace at all times and in every way. Be by my side always.

In the name of Jesus, amen.

As much as it is possible, live in peace with everyone.

Romans 12:18 GW

Blessed are those who make peace.
They will be called God's children.

Matthew 5:9 GW

You will keep the man in perfect peace whose mind is kept on You, because he trusts in You.

Isaiah 26:3 NLV

Do not worry. Learn to pray about everything. Give thanks to God as you ask Him for what you need. The peace of God is much greater than the human mind can understand. This peace will keep your hearts and minds through Christ Jesus.

Philippians 4:6–7 NLV

May the Lord of peace give you his peace at all times and in every way. The Lord be with all of you.

2 Thessalonians 3:16 GW

Perplexed

Dear Lord,

Life and all its trials and decisions can be perplexing. How do I know what to do? How do I know which way to turn, especially when I am fenced in with troubles and difficulties?

You cover me when I am perplexed. You help me when I am unsure of what to think or do about the problems in my life.

When I am pressed down, surrounded by troubles, I am not crushed. When I am perplexed by my circumstances, I am not driven to despair. When I am hunted down by the enemy, I am never abandoned by God. When I am knocked down, I am not destroyed.

Because You are the answer to my every question, I will trust You completely and not rely on my own opinions. With all my heart I will rely on You to guide me, and You will lead me in every decision I make.

The fear of You is wisdom. Turning my back on my own evil thoughts and deeds shows I have real understanding.

Open my ears to wisdom. Help me to turn my heart to understanding as I cry out to know right from wrong. I lift my voice and ask You to help me understand. I look for Your wisdom as one would look for silver and hidden riches.

As I learn to regard You with worship and honor, You will show me everything I need to know.

In the name of Jesus, amen.

We are pressed on every side by troubles, but we are not crushed. We are perplexed, but not driven to despair. We are hunted down, but never abandoned by God. We get knocked down, but we are not destroyed.

> 2 Corinthians 4:8–9 NLT

> Trust in the Lord completely,
> and do not rely on your own opinions.
> With all your heart rely on him to guide you,
> and he will lead you in every decision you make.
>
> Proverbs 3:5 TPT

> The fear of the Lord is true wisdom;
> to forsake evil is real understanding.
>
> Job 28:28 NLT

Make your ear open to wisdom. Turn your heart to understanding. If you cry out to know right from wrong, and lift your voice for understanding; if you look for her as silver, and look for her as hidden riches; then you will understand the fear of the Lord, and find what is known of God.

> Proverbs 2:2–5 NLV

Powerless

Dear Lord,

How powerless I feel, which is why I need to look to You always!

You are the remedy for my weakness. Help me to be strong as I look to You and Your strength; keep me strong as I keep my eyes on You.

The best news is that I do not have to be powerless because I can receive power from the Holy Spirit, who will fill my soul and anoint me with the power of Christ.

Lord, I call and You answer. You fill me with Your presence and make me bold and strong of spirit. You do not give me a spirit of fear but of power, of love, and of a good, sound mind. I receive Your Spirit and trust You. I receive Your power, Your love, and Your might for strength of mind.

You have told me to be strong and to have strength of heart. This I can do when I stay in You. I have no need to fear or lose faith, for You are in me; You are with me wherever I go.

Even when I find myself in lack or in a tight situation, You give me contentment. Whether I'm fed or hungry, with or without, I am content because Your Spirit is in me. You and Your Spirit provide my power and strength.

In the name of Jesus, amen.

Look to the Lord and ask for His strength. Look to Him all the time.

1 Chronicles 16:11 NLV

But you will receive power when the Holy Spirit comes into your life.

Acts 1:8 NLV

When I called, you answered me.
You made me bold by strengthening my soul.

Psalm 138:3 GW

For God did not give us a spirit of fear. He gave us a spirit of power and of love and of a good mind.

2 Timothy 1:7 NLV

Have I not told you? Be strong and have strength of heart! Do not be afraid or lose faith. For the Lord your God is with you anywhere you go.

Joshua 1:9 NLV

I know how to survive in tight situations, and I know how to enjoy having plenty. In fact, I have learned how to face any circumstances: fed or hungry, with or without. I can be content in any and every situation through the Anointed One who is my power and strength.

Philippians 4:12–13 VOICE

Prayerful

Dear Lord,

You have called me to make my life a prayer, to always talk to You about my thoughts, feelings, concerns, needs, and troubles.

How wonderful that I have a direct channel to You and that I never need to worry that You see me as an interruption. You always have time for me because You are outside of time.

I do not need to be anxious about anything because I can bring everything to You. You long to hear from me and to listen to my requests. You want me to tell You about my needs. And my response to your invitation is to thank You for everything. I thank You right now!

How wonderful that You hear me when I call to You for help. You hear my call and rescue me from every trouble.

May we, Your people, wake up and call Your name. Help us to put our pride away and to look into Your face. Help us to turn from our sinful ways. When we do that, You will answer. You will forgive our sins and heal our land. So we urgently seek You and ask that You heal our land now.

I bring this and all the things on my heart to You because I know that whatever I ask from You and believe I will receive, You will give to me.

Give me the vision to ask, and give me the faith to believe.

In the name of Jesus, amen.

Make your life a prayer.

1 Thessalonians 5:17 TPT

Don't be anxious about things; instead, pray. Pray about everything. He longs to hear your requests, so talk to God about your needs and be thankful for what has come.

Philippians 4:6 VOICE

The LORD hears his people when they call to him
for help.
He rescues them from all their troubles.

Psalm 34:17 NLT

If My people who are called by My name put away their pride and pray, and look for My face, and turn from their sinful ways, then I will hear from heaven. I will forgive their sin, and will heal their land.

2 Chronicles 7:14 NLV

So listen to what I'm saying: Whatever you pray for or ask from God, believe that you'll receive it and you will.

Mark 11:24 VOICE

Regret

Dear Lord,

I haven't won my race yet, but I praise You because I'm still running! So I pledge to keep running as I lengthen my stride. I run straight toward the goal to win the prize that You offer in Christ Jesus.

As I run this race, I will give You all my worries about my past mistakes as well as my missteps. I find it amazing that You want to carry the weight of these regrets because You care about me.

Sometimes I think I've discovered shortcuts, but when I get off track I trip and fall. Sometimes I stumble when my way is rocky. But you are there to pull me to my feet.

But even when I fall flat on my face, You do not reject me. You use these times to teach me more about Your grace because You are powerful enough to allow my missteps to be part of my journey to You. Looking back, I see it's all for my good.

You allow me to help others who stumble over the pitfalls that tripped me. Because I belong to You, You make every step and misstep a part of my race.

So, Lord, right now, I give You all my regrets and ask that You turn each one of them into a miracle of Your love and grace. Let me use my regrets as a way to serve You as I continue to run into Your arms.

In the name of Jesus, amen.

I can't consider myself a winner yet. This is what I do: I don't look back, I lengthen my stride, and I run straight toward the goal to win the prize that God's heavenly call offers in Christ Jesus. Whoever has a mature faith should think this way. And if you think differently, God will show you how to think.

Philippians 3:13–15 GW

Give all your worries and cares to God, for he cares about you.

1 Peter 5:7 NLT

Within your heart you can make plans for your future,
but the Lord chooses the steps you take to get there.

Proverbs 16:9 TPT

And we know that in all things God works for the good of those who love him, who have been called according to his purpose.

Romans 8:28 NIV

Come back to the place of safety,
all you prisoners who still have hope!
I promise this very day
that I will repay two blessings for each of your
troubles.

Zechariah 9:12 NLT

Remorse

Dear Lord,

Though my spirit belongs to You, I still make mistakes. When I fail, I know that I can come to You and confess my sins. I battle my selfish desires as I continue to realize that all of me belongs to You. You have called me to be a temple where Your Holy Spirit rests. This means I no longer belong to myself.

I was bought with a price, so help me to glorify You in the way I use my body and care for it. It's not a sin to be out of shape, but I realize that being out of shape does not honor You.

I repent from the mistakes I've willfully and carelessly made and turn back to You so that my sins may be wiped out and so that I can be refreshed. Fill me with the gift of Your Holy Spirit.

Jesus, thank You for the gift of remorse. Thank You that now that I have repented and turned back to You, You have refreshed my spirit and restored our relationship.

My repentance and baptism with water represents that you have forgiven my sin and have filled me with Your Holy Spirit.

I embrace Your message of forgiveness. I know that I will never face Your condemnation because I am in You. You have raised me from death to eternal life.

In the name of Jesus, amen.

Don't you know that your body is a temple that belongs to the Holy Spirit? The Holy Spirit, whom you received from God, lives in you. You don't belong to yourselves. You were bought for a price. So bring glory to God in the way you use your body.

1 Corinthians 6:19–20 GW

Repent, then, and turn to God, so that your sins may be wiped out, that times of refreshing may come from the Lord.

Acts 3:19 NIV

Peter replied, "Repent and be baptized, every one of you, in the name of Jesus Christ for the forgiveness of your sins. And you will receive the gift of the Holy Spirit."

Acts 2:38 NIV

I speak to you an eternal truth: if you embrace my message and believe in the One who sent me, you will never face condemnation, for in me, you have already passed from the realm of death into the realm of eternal life!

John 5:24 TPT

Sad

ear Lord,
    Sometimes my soul is troubled with sadness. But because You are my help and my God, I know that I can praise You anyway. I call out to You, and You answer me.

Things happen in life that are sad, and at times my sadness is an appropriate emotion. However, when that sadness won't quit or when a dark spirit tries to chain my heart to despair, it's time to place myself under Your authority. It's time to shoo that dark spirit away. So I say to any dark spirit trying to attach itself to my emotions, "Shoo! Leave now in the power and authority of the name and the blood of Jesus. I revoke any agreement I may have made with you that allows you to torment me."

Lord, I also know that You never place darkness into my soul because You give me the light of Your presence. You allow me to trade my ashes for a crown of beauty, my sorrow for the oil of joy, the spirit of hopelessness for the spirit of praise. I make that trade now!

Because of all You've done for me, I will be like a beautiful oak tree planted by You.

Fill my mind with beauty and truth instead of darkness or dark media. Lead me to meditate on those things that are honorable, right, pure, lovely, good, virtuous, and praiseworthy.

My sadness will dissolve, and I will praise You for the joy You have restored to my life.

In the name of Jesus, amen.

Why are you sad, O my soul? Why have you become troubled within me? Hope in God, for I will yet praise Him, my help and my God.

Psalm 42:11 NLV

In my distress I called to the LORD,
and he answered me.

Jonah 2:2 NIV

So place yourselves under God's authority. Resist the devil, and he will run away from you.

James 4:7 GW

To those who have sorrow in Zion I will give them a crown of beauty instead of ashes. I will give them the oil of joy instead of sorrow, and a spirit of praise instead of a spirit of no hope. Then they will be called oaks that are right with God, planted by the Lord, that He may be honored.

Isaiah 61:3 NLV

Finally, brothers and sisters, fill your minds with beauty and truth. Meditate on whatever is honorable, whatever is right, whatever is pure, whatever is lovely, whatever is good, whatever is virtuous and praiseworthy.

Philippians 4:8 VOICE

Self-Conscious

*D*ear Lord,

I hate it when I am self-conscious, when I feel as if everyone is looking at and judging me. That's when I want to run and hide!

Your Word reminds me that fearing others is a dangerous trap but trusting You means safety.

Help me not to be afraid of the faces that look my way, for I know that You will deliver me from being self-conscious.

I will always keep my eyes on You. With You beside me, I cannot be shaken.

You are my helper, so what do I have to fear? There is nothing anyone can do to me, no judgment or wrongdoing on their part that could ever take me out of Your hand.

So, Lord, I've decided that I want to push back against the fear that has kept me from doing all that You are calling me to do. In exchange for my self-consciousness, I ask that You wrap me in Your perfect love, for when I am wearing Your love, fear has no way to attach itself to me.

Besides, my focus shouldn't be on myself anyway. My focus should be on You and the love You have put into my heart for others.

When I am living in Your light, it's easy for me to have fellowship with others. And as for others judging me, I have nothing to fear. You have already cleansed me from all sin.

In the name of Jesus, amen.

Fearing people is a dangerous trap,
but trusting the LORD means safety.

Proverbs 29:25 NLT

"Do not be afraid of their faces, for I am with you to deliver you,"
says the LORD.

Jeremiah 1:8 NKJV

I keep my eyes always on the LORD.
With him at my right hand, I will not be shaken.

Psalm 16:8 NIV

So we can confidently say,

"The Lord is my helper;
I will not fear;
what can man do to me?"

Hebrews 13:6 ESV

No fear exists where his love is. Rather, perfect love gets rid of
fear, because fear involves punishment. The person who lives in
fear doesn't have perfect love.

1 John 4:18 GW

But if we are living in the light, as God is in the light, then we
have fellowship with each other, and the blood of Jesus, his Son,
cleanses us from all sin.

1 John 1:7 NLT

Selfish

Dear Lord,

How many times have I imagined how much better my life would be if only I had more—more money, more things, more attention, more power, or more than my neighbors? How many times have I pushed and shoved to get more instead of praising You for what You've already given me?

I am sorry. Please direct my heart to Your Word rather than to get-rich-quick schemes.

You have blessed me. I should trust You, not my bank account, which has already betrayed me a time or two. You richly give me what I need.

Lead me to use my money to do good, being rich in good works and generous to those in need, always ready to share with others.

I can't take my earthly possessions to heaven with me, so why do I strive to get even more junk? I would do far better to serve others, ensuring that You will provide treasures for me in heaven.

You will bless me when I give, for it's not true that You help those who help themselves. Instead, You help those who help others.

Teach me to be concerned about not just my own well-being but the well-being of others. Let me be devoted to those you have put into my life so that we can become a loving family, showing love and kindness as well as respect to one another.

In the name of Jesus, amen.

Direct my heart toward your written instructions
rather than getting rich in underhanded ways.

Psalm 119:36 GW

Teach those who are rich in this world not to be proud and not to trust in their money, which is so unreliable. Their trust should be in God, who richly gives us all we need for our enjoyment. Tell them to use their money to do good. They should be rich in good works and generous to those in need, always being ready to share with others. By doing this they will be storing up their treasure as a good foundation for the future so that they may experience true life.

1 Timothy 6:17–19 NLT

The man who gives much will have much, and he who helps others will be helped himself.

Proverbs 11:25 NLV

People should be concerned about others and not just about themselves.

1 Corinthians 10:24 GW

Be devoted to each other like a loving family. Excel in showing respect for each other.

Romans 12:10 GW

Shamed

Dear Lord,

When I feel shamed, I look to Jesus, the founder and perfecter of my faith. How remarkable that He found joy in enduring the cross, in bearing its shame for my sake. Because Jesus bore my shame, He will lift my shame off me whenever I ask.

I'm asking now, because Your Word says that anyone who believes in You will never be put to shame.

I confess my sins that caused my shame. I know that through You I am forgiven. I know that You have cleansed me from all that I've done wrong.

As I give You my shame, I know that You will remove even the stigma of my shame.

And that's it. My sin is gone, covered, meaning my shame has disappeared. The case is closed.

Because of Your work on the cross, no one can accuse me because I am joined in a life-union with You, Jesus.

Because I've turned to You, not only have You freed me from my shame, You've also given me radiant joy. My face will no longer bear the shadow of disgrace. When people see me, they can whisper about my past if they'd like, but it's all meaningless because that is not who I am anymore. I am Yours. I am forgiven, and I am shame-free.

In the name of Jesus, amen.

Looking to Jesus, the founder and perfecter of our faith, who for the joy that was set before him endured the cross, despising the shame, and is seated at the right hand of the throne of God.

Hebrews 12:2 ESV

As Scripture says, "Anyone who believes in him will never be put to shame."

Romans 10:11 NIV

God is faithful and reliable. If we confess our sins, he forgives them and cleanses us from everything we've done wrong.

1 John 1:9 GW

So now the case is closed. There remains no accusing voice of condemnation against those who are joined in life-union with Jesus, the Anointed One.

Romans 8:1 TPT

I prayed to the LORD, and he answered me.
   He freed me from all my fears.
Those who look to him for help will be radiant with joy;
   no shadow of shame will darken their faces.

Psalm 34:4–5 NLT

Shocked

Dear Lord,

How can I not be shocked by what happened? But just because it was so unexpected doesn't mean You have forgotten me. You will soon come to my rescue. You will get me through this.

I have hope because I have experienced Your great mercy before. I will not be wiped out, because You will wipe away my tears.

I can count on Your unlimited compassion, which arrives fresh every morning. Great is Your faithfulness.

I will not yield to fear because I know that You are near. I know that You never turn Your gaze from me because You are my faithful God. You infuse me with Your strength and help me to survive and thrive in every situation. Soon, You will hold my hand high in victory! But for now, You are holding my hand tight, and You won't let go.

That's why I will not be afraid of the terrors of the night or the arrows that fly in the day. I will not dread disease that stalks in darkness, nor will I fear disaster that strikes at midday.

Because I am listening to You, I can live without worry. I can be free from the dread of any disaster that has fallen.

You care for me and carry me when disaster strikes. You carry me through it all. I am safe in Your arms.

In the name of Jesus, amen.

The reason I can still find hope is that I keep this one
	thing in mind:
the Lord's mercy.
		We were not completely wiped out.
		His compassion is never limited.
			It is new every morning.
			His faithfulness is great.
				Lamentations 3:21–23 GW

Do not yield to fear, for I am always near.
	Never turn your gaze from me, for I am your faithful
		God.
	I will infuse you with my strength
	and help you in every situation.
	I will hold you firmly with my victorious right hand.
				Isaiah 41:10 TPT

Do not be afraid of the terrors of the night,
	nor the arrow that flies in the day.
Do not dread the disease that stalks in darkness,
	nor the disaster that strikes at midday.
				Psalm 91:5–6 NLT

But whoever listens to me will live without worry
	and will be free from the dread of disaster.
				Proverbs 1:33 GW

Since God cares for you, let Him carry all your burdens and
worries.

				1 Peter 5:7 VOICE

Stressed

Dear Lord,

You have given me the gift of peace straight from Your heart to mine. This peace is not fragile, like the peace the world gives, but solid, strong, and perfect. It is a peace I can wear daily, and it never wears out.

Since I have access to peace like this, why should I yield to fear or let my heart be troubled? Give me the faith to be courageous so that I will not lose my peace.

When my stressors arise, I will call to You, and You will answer me and set me free from a stress reaction. You will remind me that I already possess Your wonderful and beautiful peace. Knowing this, I will slip Your peace on. I will wear it in front of all my stressors, and stress will have no choice but to disappear.

Lord, You are on my side, and I do not need to panic or fear or get stressed out. Stress or stressful people cannot harm me.

I will entrust all my ways to You. I will trust You, knowing that You will act on my behalf.

Therefore, I stand firm in the face of all my stresses and stressors. When I do this, I win the prize of peace, for You are the God of peace, and You will quickly crush Satan under my feet.

Thank You that Your good will is with me.

In the name of Jesus, amen.

I leave the gift of peace with you—my peace. Not the kind of fragile peace given by the world, but my perfect peace. Don't yield to fear or be troubled in your hearts—instead, be courageous!

John 14:27 TPT

> During times of trouble I called on the LORD.
>> The LORD answered me and set me free from all
>>> of them.
>
> The LORD is on my side.
>> I am not afraid.
>>> What can mortals do to me?

Psalm 118:5–6 GW

> Entrust your ways to the LORD.
> Trust him, and he will act on your behalf.

Psalm 37:5 GW

Stand firm, and you will win life.

Luke 21:19 NIV

The God of peace will quickly crush Satan under your feet. May the good will of our Lord Jesus be with you!

Romans 16:20 GW

Strife

Dear Lord,

Here we go again. Did You hear what he said? Did You see what she did? I'd like to give them a piece of my mind.

But wait. You would have me choose peace of mind instead.

I'm taking a deep breath and stepping back from the fight because You have called me to make peace my top priority. Instead of instructing me to butt heads, You instruct me to stand down. As I do, You will help me to initiate peace and encourage those You put in my life.

Your Word warns me to have nothing to do with foolish talk or arguments, which can lead to trouble. So I will work to bypass trouble by serving others with kindness, even if I have to suffer for doing good.

So help me to be gentle when You call me to explain those things that people don't want to hear, for You may change their hearts so that they turn to the truth.

I can have more peace when I stop my complaining and arguing and avoid quarrels. Any fool can start a fight, but only a person of wisdom can avoid a conflict.

The best remedy You have given me for avoiding strife, quarrels, and hurt feelings is to love. As I love others with Your love, Your love will cover every wrong.

In the name of Jesus, amen.

So then, make it your top priority to live a life of peace with harmony in your relationships, eagerly seeking to strengthen and encourage one another.

Romans 14:19 TPT

Let me say it again. Have nothing to do with foolish talk and those who want to argue. It can only lead to trouble. A servant owned by God must not make trouble. He must be kind to everyone. He must be able to teach. He must be willing to suffer when hurt for doing good. Be gentle when you try to teach those who are against what you say. God may change their hearts so they will turn to the truth.

2 Timothy 2:23–25 NLV

Do everything without complaining or arguing.

Philippians 2:14 GW

Avoiding a quarrel is honorable.
After all, any stubborn fool can start a fight.
Proverbs 20:3 GW

Hate starts quarrels,
but love covers every wrong
Proverbs 10:12 GW

Strong

ear Lord,
Sometimes I look at my problems and wonder if I'm strong enough to endure them all, but I have a secret weapon. I can continually seek Your strength.

I'm sorry when I'm impatient, because You always flex Your muscles and do the heavy lifting. You are always right on time—never too early and never too late.

You are my strength and my song, for You have given me victory time and again. You are my God, and I will praise You and exalt You.

It's interesting to contrast who You are (the strong one) with who I am (the weak one). In fact, if You weren't the muscle behind my many victories, I would have zero wins. But You hear my cry, and You always help me conquer even impossible dilemmas.

I'm not sure how You manage to do all You do for me, but You once said, "My grace is sufficient for you, for My power is made perfect in weakness." I am strong in You when I am weak. As the apostle Paul explained, Your strength was the very reason he delighted in his weaknesses, insults, hardships, persecutions, and difficulties, because when he faced such trials, he became strong in You.

I agree that "I can do all things because Christ gives me the strength." This is a wonder, a miracle, and a marvel, and I will praise You for all You have done for me.

In the name of Jesus, amen.

Seek the Lord and his strength;
  seek his presence continually!
        1 Chronicles 16:11 ESV

Wait with hope for the Lord.
Be strong, and let your heart be courageous.
Yes, wait with hope for the Lord.

                    Psalm 27:14 GW

The Lord is my strength and my song;
  he has given me victory.
This is my God, and I will praise him—
  my father's God, and I will exalt him!

                    Exodus 15:2 NLT

But he said to me, "My grace is sufficient for you, for my power is made perfect in weakness." Therefore I will boast all the more gladly about my weaknesses, so that Christ's power may rest on me. That is why, for Christ's sake, I delight in weaknesses, in insults, in hardships, in persecutions, in difficulties. For when I am weak, then I am strong.

                    2 Corinthians 12:9–11 NIV

I can do all things because Christ gives me the strength.

                    Philippians 4:13 NLV

Suffering

Dear Lord,

It's easier to be happy about the tests I've completed than to be happy about the tests I'm currently going through. But then I remember that You will use my current difficulty to build my faith as long as I don't give up.

So help me to make it through this difficulty in Your power, grace, and mercy. If the difficulty continues, I will wait on You, trusting that You are moving on my behalf. Much of my suffering will be relieved if I will only trust in You. When I learn how to wait on You in trust, I will be strong and complete and will have everything I need.

The good news about my suffering is that it creates endurance, which creates character, which creates confidence as Your love pours into my heart through the power of the Holy Spirit. What I am going through is insignificant compared to the glory You will soon reveal to me.

And thank You for supplying me with Your continued peace. I am confident I can rest in You even as this trial runs its course.

With great hope, I realize that You are the one who conquered the world, so this current trial is not too big for You to handle.

I want to continue to trust in You in hope, and in Your strength. I know this suffering will end and that You will use it in miraculous ways. Thank You.

In the name of Jesus, amen.

My Christian brothers, you should be happy when you have all kinds of tests. You know these prove your faith. It helps you not to give up. Learn well how to wait so you will be strong and complete and in need of nothing.

James 1:2–4 NLV

But that's not all. We also brag when we are suffering. We know that suffering creates endurance, endurance creates character, and character creates confidence. We're not ashamed to have this confidence, because God's love has been poured into our hearts by the Holy Spirit, who has been given to us.

Romans 5:3–5 GW

I consider our present sufferings insignificant compared to the glory that will soon be revealed to us.

Romans 8:18 GW

The peace which is in me will be in you and will give you great confidence as you rest in me. For in this unbelieving world you will experience trouble and sorrows, but you must be courageous, for I have conquered the world!

John 16:33 TPT

Suicidal

Dear Lord,

In this dark and painful night, You are with me.

The enemy whispers lies of death, but You whisper words of life. You ask me to choose life so that my descendants and I will live.

You created my life and call me to live because You have a purpose for me that I have yet to fulfill. If I trust that my times are in Your hands, I will live to find that purpose because You are the God who loves me.

Even in my despair, You tell me that Your grace is enough. You promise to give me Your power in my weakness, so please give me Your power now.

I give my heart to You and know that even my body belongs to You. May Your Spirit fill my heart and empower me to choose life.

The enemy tempts me to shut the door to my future. But I reject his lies, knowing You hold my future, a future filled with hope. I will trust You and give You the broken pieces of my life if only to watch what You can do with them.

So I will wait for You, Lord, as You move on my behalf. Be with me while I wait, for You are my help and my shield. You will help me to find joy as I learn how to trust You in every circumstance. May Your mercy rest on me as I wait in hope for You.

In the name of Jesus, amen.

Choose life so that you and your descendants will live.

Deuteronomy 30:19 GW

But I trust in you, O LORD;
I say, "You are my God."
My times are in your hand.

Psalm 31:14–15 ESV

But he said to me, "My grace is sufficient for you, for my power is made perfect in weakness." Therefore I will boast all the more gladly about my weaknesses, so that Christ's power may rest on me.

2 Corinthians 12:9 NIV

Don't you know that your body is a temple that belongs to the Holy Spirit? The Holy Spirit, whom you received from God, lives in you. You don't belong to yourselves.

1 Corinthians 6:19 GW

We wait for the LORD.
He is our help and our shield.
In him our hearts find joy.
In his holy name we trust.
Let your mercy rest on us, O LORD,
since we wait with hope for you.

Psalm 33:20–22 GW

Tempted

Dear Lord,

When I focus on the things I shouldn't, my thoughts lead me to act out with wrongdoing. Please forgive me for my failings and give me the strength to change my thought life so that I can focus on good things and do what pleases You. I give my thought life to You and ask that You direct it.

Like a mom who removes dangerous objects from her toddler's reach, help me to remove those things from my life that tempt me.

As I ponder a way to break free from my sinful thought life, I realize that You understand. You sympathize with my weakness because You, Jesus, also walked this earth as a human being. You were tempted in the same ways I am tempted, with one big difference. You meditated on things above instead of on Your temptations. You walked sin-free.

Because You understand what I'm going through, You are able to give me the strength, and a plan to change my thought life whenever I am tempted. Remind me that I can call a friend, pray, read Your Word, leave the room, log off, run an errand, or change the channel.

I'm comforted by the fact that the temptations I experience are much the same as the temptations that others have conquered through You.

Lord, You are faithful. When I turn my eyes from what is tempting me and focus on You, You will make a way of escape.

In the name of Jesus, amen.

A man is tempted to do wrong when he lets himself be led by what his bad thoughts tell him to do.

James 1:14 NLV

Keep away from everything that even looks like sin.

1 Thessalonians 5:22 NLV

We have a chief priest who is able to sympathize with our weaknesses. He was tempted in every way that we are, but he didn't sin.

Hebrews 4:15 GW

Because Jesus experienced temptation when he suffered, he is able to help others when they are tempted.

Hebrews 2:18 GW

You have never been tempted to sin in any different way than other people. God is faithful. He will not allow you to be tempted more than you can take. But when you are tempted, He will make a way for you to keep from falling into sin.

1 Corinthians 10:13 NLV

Troubled

Dear Lord,

I am troubled, and You are the only one I can turn to. As I call out to You, even before I finish telling You what's wrong, You hear me and answer. You tell me that I am Yours. So I give my troubles to You and trust that You know what to do with them. Your plan will certainly be better than mine. I choose to trust You now, even though I don't understand what You're up to.

You are a good and a safe place where I can hide in times of trouble. Because I run to You, You open the door to me so I can hide in your safety.

I give myself to You, God. As I do, the devil sees You and runs away. He flees not because he's afraid of me but because he knows better than to tangle with me when I am in You.

Even though my troubles are many, I will wait on You. I will be strong in You, and You will encourage my heart.

You give me peace because You have overcome the world. I ask that Christ's peace control me, for You have called me into this peace through my friendship with You. You have also called me into fellowship with those who believe in You.

Help me to be thankful so that my discouragement and fear will lift and my mind will be free to trust You.

In the name of Jesus, amen.

Before they even call out to me,
    I will answer them;
    before they've finished telling me what they need,
    I'll have already heard.

Isaiah 65:24 TPT

The Lord is good, a safe place in times of trouble. And He knows those who come to Him to be safe.

Nahum 1:7 NLV

I've told you this so that my peace will be with you. In the world you'll have trouble. But cheer up! I have overcome the world.

John 16:33 GW

So give yourselves to God. Stand against the devil and he will run away from you.

James 4:7 NLV

Wait with hope for the LORD.
    Be strong, and let your heart be courageous.
    Yes, wait with hope for the LORD.

Psalm 27:14 GW

Also, let Christ's peace control you. God has called you into this peace by bringing you into one body. Be thankful.

Colossians 3:15 GW

Trusting

Dear Lord,

I have spent a lot of time in fear, afraid of the future, the past, and the present. Sometimes I'm even terrified that You won't come to my rescue.

But I've got it all wrong. You're the one who holds on to me, and You'll never let go. All I need to do is leave my fears with You, for You can turn the plans of the enemy into miracles.

I will save myself from so much anxiety when I finally realize that You are trustworthy. With You on my side, no one can knock me down, no one can take me out of Your hand or remove Your love from me.

Yes, I can trust You. You never back away from me. Instead, You open Your arms wide.

I will trust You with all my heart. I will stop trying to figure out what to do about my problems and seek You. You will show me the direction You want me to take. You will make things come together for the good.

You will keep me in perfect peace through whatever I go through. I will keep my thoughts on You and will trust You always, for You are my God, my eternal Rock.

I dedicate my every step to You. I know that You will help me and will answer my every prayer.

In the name of Jesus, amen.

But when I am afraid,
   I will put my trust in you.
I praise God for what he has promised.
   I trust in God, so why should I be afraid?
   What can mere mortals do to me?

Psalm 56:3–4 NLT

Those who know your name trust in you,
   for you, Lord, have never forsaken those
      who seek you.

Psalm 9:10 NIV

Trust in the LORD with all your heart;
   do not depend on your own understanding.
Seek his will in all you do,
   and he will show you which path to take.

Proverbs 3:5–6 NLT

You will keep in perfect peace
   all who trust in you,
   all whose thoughts are fixed on you!
Trust in the LORD always,
   for the LORD God is the eternal Rock.

Isaiah 26:3–4 NLT

Give your way over to the Lord. Trust in Him also.
   And He will do it.

Psalm 37:5 NLV

Unworthy

Dear Lord,

I am trembling before You, ashamed to call out to You in prayer. I am not worthy to come into Your presence. Then I remember Jesus, the one who loves me, the one who died in my place. I'm not wearing my own filthy rags when I come before You; I'm wearing the beautiful righteousness of Jesus.

So why am I so afraid of You? You are the one who loves me, the one who is always with me! You are my hero who saves me as You rejoice over me. Your love for me is never stale but always fresh. You celebrate me with joy.

You have compassion for me, just like a dad who loves his kids. You know that I am only flesh because You created me from dust.

You understand that I am weak and flawed, but You, Jesus, are strong. You were also tested in the same ways I am. But You emerged victorious, without failing God. I can stand boldly before Him because I am standing in Your unending supply of mercy and grace.

You are merciful and compassionate. You don't view me in anger for my failures. You see me through eyes of unfailing love. You are good to me, and You shower me with kindness. Give me the boldness to realize who I am in Christ—worthy, loved, and forgiven.

In the name of Jesus, amen.

The LORD your God is with you.
He is a hero who saves you.
He happily rejoices over you,
renews you with his love,
and celebrates over you with shouts of joy.

Zephaniah 3:17 GW

The LORD is like a father to his children,
tender and compassionate to those who fear him.
For he knows how weak we are;
he remembers we are only dust.

Psalm 103:13–14 NLT

For Jesus is not some high priest who has no sympathy for our weaknesses and flaws. He has already been tested in every way that we are tested; but He emerged victorious, without failing God. So let us step boldly to the throne of grace, where we can find mercy and grace to help when we need it most.

Hebrews 4:15–16 VOICE

The LORD is merciful and compassionate,
slow to get angry and filled with unfailing love.
The LORD is good to everyone.
He showers compassion on all his creation.

Psalm 145:8–9 NLT

Victorious

Dear Lord,

As I prepare for battle, I am amazed to realize that You, the Lord my God, go into battle with me. You will fight against my enemies, and You will give me victory through Jesus Christ my Lord.

I will sing my victory song now, as I praise You for who You are and what You mean to me.

Because I am in You, I have been reborn through the work of Jesus, who died for the forgiveness of my sins. Because this is true and because I have faith in You, I have the victory over the whole world.

So, yes, I do believe. I believe that You are the one who fights my battles and the one who wins the war. I am the one who worships and adores You.

You give me overwhelming victories in all my troubles. Nothing can separate me from Your love. Not trouble, distress, persecution, hunger, nakedness, danger, or even violent death can pull me away from You or Your love.

I belong to You because I am Your dear child. This means that I have already won a victory over all who would come against me. I have already won because I am empowered by Your Holy Spirit, who lives in me, for greater is the Holy Spirit in me than the spirit of darkness who lives in this world.

I celebrate You, my Lord, my Savior, my warrior God. Thank You for everything.

In the name of Jesus, amen.

The Lord your God is going with you. He will fight for you against your enemies and give you victory.

Deuteronomy 20:4 GW

Thank God that he gives us the victory through our Lord Jesus Christ.

1 Corinthians 15:57 GW

Everyone who has been born from God has won the victory over the world. Our faith is what wins the victory over the world.

1 John 5:4 GW

What will separate us from the love Christ has for us? Can trouble, distress, persecution, hunger, nakedness, danger, or violent death separate us from his love? . . . The one who loves us gives us an overwhelming victory in all these difficulties.

Romans 8:35, 37 GW

But you belong to God, my dear children. You have already won a victory over those people, because the Spirit who lives in you is greater than the spirit who lives in the world.

1 John 4:4 NLT

Wayward

Dear Lord,

It seems I can't win. I can't be good enough for You. The payment for my sins will be eternal death.

Except that Your Word says I don't have to receive death in exchange for my sins. Instead, You offer me everlasting life through Jesus Christ.

This offer sounds too good to be true, but Jesus said, "I am the way, the truth, and the life. No one goes to the Father except through me."

Yes, I would very much like to take You up on this offer. And the first thing I must do is repent, meaning I must recognize that I am a sinner and turn from my sin to Jesus. If I do, Jesus will take my sin off me.

So, yes, I turn from my sin, and I turn to Jesus to be the Lord of my life.

Now I am forgiven, clean, and whole. You refresh my spirit with Your very presence. You are faithful and reliable. Because I confessed my sins to You, You have forgiven me and cleansed me from everything I've ever done wrong.

This is something I cannot be quiet about. I have to share this good news with my friends and family so that they can be delivered from the power of darkness. I will tell everyone that I now belong to You, and You will give me the power to live for You. I am now free in Christ Jesus.

In the name of Jesus, amen.

The payment for sin is death, but the gift that God freely gives is everlasting life found in Christ Jesus our Lord.

Romans 6:23 GW

Jesus answered him, "I am the way, the truth, and the life. No one goes to the Father except through me."

John 14:6 GW

And now you must repent and turn back to God so that your sins will be removed, and so that times of refreshing will stream from the Lord's presence.

Acts 3:19 TPT

God is faithful and reliable. If we confess our sins, he forgives them and cleanses us from everything we've done wrong.

1 John 1:9 GW

So, go ahead—let everyone know it!
Tell the world how he broke through
and delivered you from the power of darkness and
has gathered us together from all over the world.
He has set us free to be his very own!

Psalm 107:2–3 TPT

Weak

ear Lord,
    You are all I need. You give me grace because Your power works best in weak people—like me.

I am a weakling compared to You. But in this I take great delight because the strength of Christ's power is explosive and infuses me so that I can conquer every difficulty.

When I am in You, being weak is a blessing. Even troubles are a blessing because to win my battles, all I have to do is entrust my troubles to You.

Your Holy Spirit also helps me with my weakness. It doesn't matter that I'm not smart enough to know exactly what to pray because the Holy Spirit is praying for me in groans too deep for words.

The thing I must watch for in my weakness is temptation. The spirit in me is willing to ignore temptation, but my weak flesh would allow me to cave in. So, Lord, I call on You to give me strength in my flesh to overcome temptation. Please give me victory so that my life pleases You.

Lord, You are the one who gives me strength. You make my way perfect. You make my feet like those of a deer so that I can leap onto craggy rocks with sure footing.

Lord, You train my hands so that I can shoot arrows in battle. In You I will win every battle, for You are my strength. You are my victory.

In the name of Jesus, amen.

But he said to me, "My grace is sufficient for you, for my power is made perfect in weakness." Therefore I will boast all the more gladly about my weaknesses, so that Christ's power may rest on me.

2 Corinthians 12:9 NIV

I find that the strength of Christ's explosive power infuses me to conquer every difficulty.

Philippians 4:13 TPT

Likewise the Spirit helps us in our weakness. For we do not know what to pray for as we ought, but the Spirit himself intercedes for us with groanings too deep for words.

Romans 8:26 ESV

Watch and pray that you may not enter into temptation. The spirit indeed is willing, but the flesh is weak.

Matthew 26:41 ESV

God arms me with strength
and makes my way perfect.
He makes my feet like those of a deer
and gives me sure footing on high places.
He trains my hands for battle
so that my arms can bend an archer's bow
of bronze.

Psalm 18:32–34 GW

Worried

Dear Lord,

You are the one who rescued me and brought me back to life with Christ. I can't ignore this miracle, and in the face of worry, I must turn back to You. You have called me to focus on the things that are above—where Christ holds the highest position.

Therefore, because of Christ and because You care for me, I give You all my worries and cares. I give them to You as a gift, a gift You desire.

You do not want me to remove my focus from You and place my focus on my worries. Neither do I. I worship You, not my worries. I need to focus on Your greatness instead of the things You've already taken care of.

So I will not worry about my life, or what I will eat or drink, or what I will wear, because life is more important than food and my body is more important than clothes. You will make sure these needs are cared for.

And besides, I am convinced that You will provide for my every need out of Your abundant riches of glory through Your Anointed One, Jesus Christ.

You have plans for me, and You do not want my worries to distract or sidetrack me. And I don't want to miss Your plans, which are for peace, not disaster. They are plans to give me a future filled with hope.

In the name of Jesus, amen.

Since you were brought back to life with Christ, focus on the things that are above—where Christ holds the highest position.

Colossians 3:1 GW

Give all your worries and cares to God, for he cares about you.

1 Peter 5:7 NLT

I tell you this: Do not worry about your life. Do not worry about what you are going to eat and drink. Do not worry about what you are going to wear. Is not life more important than food? Is not the body more important than clothes?

Matthew 6:25 NLV

I am convinced that my God will fully satisfy every need you have, for I have seen the abundant riches of glory revealed to me through the Anointed One, Jesus Christ!

Philippians 4:19 TPT

I know the plans that I have for you, declares the LORD. They are plans for peace and not disaster, plans to give you a future filled with hope.

Jeremiah 29:11 GW

Worshipful

Dear Lord,
   I will sing to You. I will worship You for all the wonderful things You have done for me.

From this moment on, I realize that worshiping You, Father God, isn't a matter of location but a matter of my heart. As an act of worship, I submit my heart to You, made clean through the power of Your forgiveness of sin, a place Your Holy Spirit can rest.

You, God, are a Spirit, and You long for me to mingle my heart with Yours through worship. You long for me to adore You in the realm of Spirit and truth.

So I worship You now. I worship You in a deeper way as I present my body as a living sacrifice to You. May my body be holy and acceptable to You.

I praise You in Your holy place, Your mighty heavens. I praise You for Your mighty acts and for saving me for Yourself. I praise You for Your immense greatness. I worship You with the sound of horns and harps. I worship You with tambourines and dancing. I worship You with stringed instruments and flutes and loud cymbals.

I praise You with all my heart, with all my strength, and with all my mind. May everything that has breath praise You, Lord.

Hallelujah!

In the name of Jesus, amen.

Sing to the LORD, for he has done wonderful things.

Isaiah 12:5 NLT

From here on, worshiping the Father will not be a matter of the right place but with the right heart. For God is a Spirit, and he longs to have sincere worshipers who worship and adore him in the realm of the Spirit and in truth.

John 4:23–24 TPT

Present your bodies as a living sacrifice, holy and acceptable to God, which is your spiritual worship.

Romans 12:1 ESV

Hallelujah!
Praise God in his holy place.
Praise him in his mighty heavens.
Praise him for his mighty acts.
Praise him for his immense greatness.
Praise him with sounds from horns.
Praise him with harps and lyres.
Praise him with tambourines and dancing.
Praise him with stringed instruments and flutes.
Praise him with loud cymbals.
Praise him with crashing cymbals.
Let everything that breathes praise the LORD!
Hallelujah!

Psalm 150 GW

Conclusion

I know the LORD is always with me.
I will not be shaken, for he is right beside me.

Psalm 16:8 NLT

I am a different person at the end of this writing than I was at the beginning, transformed by the power of the Word as I prayed and wrote these pages.

The themes of God's love and His promises to empower us in both our lives and emotions are truly phenomenal.

I felt His power as I explored the Scriptures and walked into deeper peace and felt deeper love for God and those He placed in my life. My prayer for You, my dear readers, is that You will also feel this same transformation power.

You are loved, and no matter what is happening in Your life, God is there. Trust Him, and you will see His beauty and feel His peace.

It is well with my soul. May it also be well with your soul.

I love you!

Dear Lord,

Your promises of love and care for me are amazing. Your call to trust You is profound. Your promises to empower me with Your Spirit are wondrous.

You are my God, and I belong to You. I pledge that despite my circumstances I will remember that You love me and that You are working everything out for my good. I pledge to trust You in the no-matter-whats of life.

Empower me by Your Spirit to overcome.

In the name of Jesus, amen.

A Gift to My Readers

I loved writing these prayers so much that I wrote too many to fit into the pages of this book. I have over a dozen prayers that I'd love to give to you as a gift. To receive my free download, please go to: www.EmotionPrayers.com.

Love,
Linda Evans Shepherd

Acknowledgments

A special thanks to my dear friend Rhonda Rhea, who suggested I write this book. Great idea! Also a special thanks to my editor Vicki Crumpton and the wonderful team at Revell of Baker Publishing Group; my brilliant agent, Janet Kobobel Grant; my dear family members, who lend me their patience and support as I write book after book; and the hundreds of women of the Advanced Writers and Speakers Association, my team of prayer warriors who have prayed for me through so many trials. I love you all! And of course, a special thanks to my Lord and Savior, Jesus Christ. You are my Rock.

Linda Evans Shepherd is an award-winning author of thirty-five books, including the bestselling *When You Don't Know What to Pray* and *When You Need to Move a Mountain* and *Empowered for Purpose.*

Linda is an internationally recognized speaker and has spoken in almost every state in the United States and in several countries around the world.

She is the president of Right to the Heart Ministries and the CEO of the Advanced Writers and Speakers Association (AWSA), which ministers to Christian women authors and speakers (www .AWSA.com and www.AWSAProtege.com). She is the publisher of *Leading Hearts* magazine (www.LeadingHearts.com) and *Arise Daily* (www.AriseDaily.com), a daily e-devotional written by the members of AWSA. She is the voice behind the *Arise Esther Movement* (www.AriseEsther.com).

Linda loves to hang out with friends and family and hubby, Paul. She is the mother of two wonderful kids, one in Austin and the other in heaven. She covets your prayers and asks that you pray for the readers of this book.

To learn more about Linda's ministries, go to www.GotToPray .com. Follow Linda on Twitter @LindaShepherd or on Facebook at LindaEvansShepherdAuthor.

Go to www.EmotionPrayers.com to sign up for a free download of additional emotion prayers.

Transform Your Life through Prayer with Linda Evans Shepherd

Visit **GotToPray.com** to receive a FREE prayer toolbox, find printable prayers, submit a prayer request, and learn more about Linda's SPEAKING and BLOGGING.

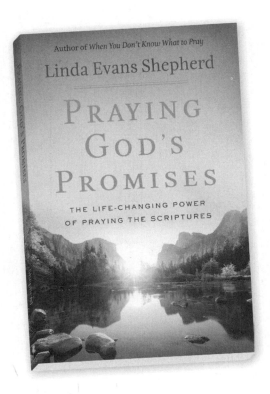

How to Bring Your Burdens to God –and Expect Answers

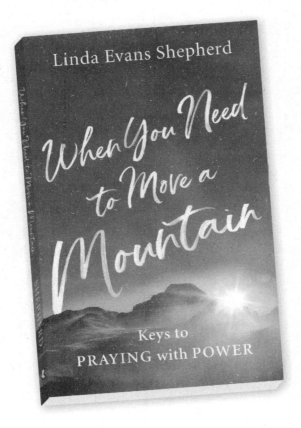

Linda Evans Shepherd

When You Need to Move a Mountain

Keys to PRAYING with POWER

In this practical and encouraging book, quickly find the specific help you need to pray for the things close to your heart. You'll also learn how to develop your own intercessory prayer battle strategy and to celebrate each victory with thanksgiving.

Ɍ Revell
a division of Baker Publishing Group
www.RevellBooks.com

Available wherever books and ebooks are sold.

BREAK FREE FROM THE CHAINS THAT HOLD YOU BACK

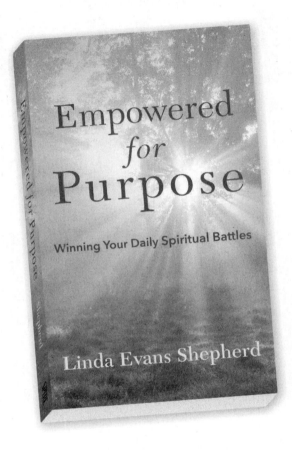

Unpacking the full armor of God, Linda Evans Shepherd offers insight into why you feel resistance when you try to find and follow your purpose and shows you how to break through your daily spiritual battles to live a victorious life.

Ꝛ Revell
a division of Baker Publishing Group
www.RevellBooks.com

Available wherever books and ebooks are sold.